The Backyard Wilderness

From the Canadian Maritimes to the Florida Keys

Vincent Abraitys

Illustrations by John Schoenherr

With a Foreword by Roger Tory Peterson

Columbia Publishing Company, Inc.
Frenchtown, New Jersey

Text copyright © 1975 by Vincent Abraitys.
Illustrations copyright © 1975 by John Schoenherr.
Foreword copyright © 1975 by Roger Tory Peterson.

No portion of this book may be reproduced in any way,
by any means, without the written permission of the publisher.
All Rights Reserved
First Printing

ISBN: 0-914366-02-5
Library of Congress Catalog Card Number: 74-80236

Manufactured in the United States of America
Book design by Laszlo Matulay

Columbia Publishing Company, Inc.
Frenchtown, New Jersey 08825

To David Fables, Robert Hirst, and James Leland Edwards—

noble companions in the field

Contents

FOREWORD BY ROGER TORY PETERSON	xiii
PREFACE	xvii

PART I THE BACKYARD WILDERNESS

A Meadow	23
A Day in May	25
Parsleys	27
The Phoebe	29
At the Portals of June	33
Warblers	34
Color in Mid-Summer	35
Hot Days	37
Horned Larks	39
Ashes and Hickories	41
Searching for Unusual Plants	45
Birds of Winter	46
The Shibboleths of Autumn	48
Murder in the Air	49

PART II SOME BASICS

Thoughts on Bird Calls and Formation Flying	53
On Avoiding Snakes	55
Never Trust a Botanist for Directions	56
Basic Equipment for Birders	60
Hawk Watching	62
Big Day	66
Rock Hounding	68
Birds Unseen but Heard	70

PART III WET PLACES

A Lesson to be Learned from a Pennsylvania Bog	75
An Abundance of Birds	76

CONTENTS

Slogging in a Pond	78
Finding a Mole Cricket	80
Dowitchers and Peeps	83
In the Field with the Hirst Brothers	85
The Shouting, Searching, Milling Throng	87
The Noblest of Wild Flowers	88
In the Great Swamp	92

PART IV FRIENDS AND FOES OF MAN

Cherries Sour and Sweet	97
Trees	99
Amanita Mushrooms	101
A Great Big Pain in the Neck	102
Owls	106
Thyme and Other Plants	107
Bats	109
Mulleins and Herbicides	113
Snakes!	115
Hawks, Swifts, and Monarch Butterflies	117
An Enormous Wasp	120

PART V FROM NORTH TO SOUTH

Birds of the Far North	125
West Virginia	126
Labrador	128
The Catskills	131
Vultures, Hawks, and Eagles in a Summer Sky	133
Plants of the Limestone Land	134
Virginia and Delaware Bay Oysters	138
A Trip Into Pine Waters	140
A Railroad for Birders and Botanists	144
In the White Mountains of New Hampshire	146
On the Delaware River	150
Springtime in Georgia and Florida	152
A Day for Rocks	155
Nova Scotia	157
Some Tough Characters	159
Holgate	160

CONTENTS

The Challenge of the Everglades and Florida	164
Cape May Point	166

PART VI THE FLOW OF LIFE

The Great Horned Owl and a Covered Bridge	171
Alive and Well	172
A Time for Ferns and Lichens	174
A Black Rail at Brigantine Refuge	178
I Meet a Pine Snake	179
Wildcat Tracks in the Snow	181
Muhlenberg's Turtle	183
Shrikes	184
The Plants of the Mid-west in the East	189
Bird Watching in the Shadow of an Airport	190
Crows	192
When the Brown Turns to Green	192

BIBLIOGRAPHY	197
INDEX	200

Illustrations

Phoebe	31
Shagbark	43
Timber Rattlesnake	57
Broad-winged Hawks	63
Mole Cricket	81
Arethusa bulbosa	89
Amanita muscaria	103
Little Brown Myotis	111
Turkey Vulture	135
Oswego River in the Pine Barrens	141
Pine Siskins	161
Lichens	175
Muhlenberg's Turtle	185
Crow	193

Foreword

Megalopolis, by usual definition, is the coastal complex centered mainly on the old highway U.S. 1, a long urban or semi-urban strip extending from Portland, Maine, to Richmond, Virginia. Town gives way to town, linked together by innumerable service stations, shopping centers, roadside restaurants, and other places of business. Inevitably, it is predicted, it will all become one great linear city.

And yet, if we probe the side roads, we quickly find ourselves in relatively wild country. Even the nearby throughways and turnpikes that take the pressure off U.S. 1 often go through great stretches of second-growth wilderness, with nary a house nor a barn in sight. My English friend, James Fisher, on his first visit to the United States in 1953, commented after we had driven some of the back roads in Massachusetts and down the elegant Merritt Parkway in Connecticut, that he was impressed by the sparseness of habitation. The paucity of agriculture and the miles and miles of woodland gave him a curious feeling of space as compared to his familiar English countryside. Large areas in my home state of Connecticut and elsewhere in the northeast have reverted from farmlands to woodlands during this century; agriculture has moved westward.

This book by Vincent Abraitys is basically about the wilderness in our backyard supplemented by excursions north to the Maritimes and south to Florida. Those who live in the seaboard states need not travel to the Far West nor to foreign lands to savor the Thoreauvian experience. It is nearby, even more accessible than when I was a youth. Indeed, there were no deer in Chautauqua County, New York, when I was a boy, nor beavers, nor wild turkeys. They are all back now and doing fine.

Nor were there Cardinals, nor Mockingbirds. These southerners have extended their ranges northward in recent years. Even Blue Jays were a rarity and to be certain of seeing one, I had to hike to Bentley's Woods or to one of the other wilder woodlots north of Jamestown. Now Jays are right in the city, as they are in a thousand other cities and towns across the land, making gluttons of themselves at the feeding tray.

On the other hand, we have witnessed the complete disappearance of the Peregrine Falcon as a breeding species in the east. We have also noted the drastic decline of the Osprey, the Bald Eagle and the Red-shouldered Hawk—all threatened by the undisciplined use of persistent pesticides

FOREWORD

such as the chlorinated hydrocarbons which, via the food chain, often build up to sub-lethal levels in some of the higher predators. Although the latter three birds may make a comeback when the ecosystem is again free of these biocides, time has run out for the eastern race of the Peregrine. It may no longer exist. Only by reintroducing hand-reared Peregrines from other parts of the world can the species ever become re-established.

To return to a more cheerful note: The message of this book is hope —flowers reborn and birds returning each Spring. And all to be seen in this wild backyard on the fringes of megalopolis. Mr. Abraitys has acted as a reporter. His columns, really short essays, which have appeared over the years in the *Hunterdon County Democrat,* may seem to lack a common denominator, a central core, but they document observations put on record as they have happened. In a way, they remind us of Thoreau's journals, bits and pieces that add up to the bold kaleidoscopic design of the four seasons.

I remember well Lee Edwards, with whom Vincent Abraitys went on so many fern hunts and warbler walks. He was a loner in a way, yet a good field companion; he was in the best tradition of what I choose to call the "old-time naturalist." Actually, for every person who could accurately name a flower or a warbler when Edwards was pioneering the woods and swamps of New Jersey, there must be a hundred who can do so now. This is a direct result of many books on natural history, field guides, Audubon lectures, and a plethora of magazine articles. The highest saturation of interest in the outdoors is undoubtedly in those communities that have a nature column in their local papers.

Measured in terms of field guides sold in bookstores, the popular interest in birds seems to be double that of wildflowers. Some of the field-glass fraternity are what might be called "listers" who activate their innate love of the hunt by spotting rarities, ticking them off on their little white checklists. I prefer the term "birder" for the devotees of this form of sport, for sport it is, rather than science. Some are almost obsessive in their pursuit of the list and we might call them "hard-core" birders. I am one of them and I defend the validity of their form of recreation. Although "bird watcher" is a useful term to cover all shades and stripes of ornithophilia, from the chickadee type of window-watcher to the academic ornithologist, the term "bird lover" I reject. Loving involves (or hopes for) reciprocation—and birds really do not reciprocate.

Butterfly-watching is now being taken up by a few lepidopterists who feel that butterflies have as much a right to fly freely as birds. The

FOREWORD

recently formed Xerces Society (named after an extinct butterfly, not the Persian King Xerxes) fosters this benign attitude.

Even flowers lend themselves to the listing game (I once listed over 200 species in one day in my home county), but most amateur botanists prefer to document their finds on Kodachrome film. Unlike birds, flowers can't evade the photographer; for this reason there are many more active flower photographers than bird photographers.

As I have written elsewhere, "Many men go through life as though they wore blinders or were sleepwalking. Their eyes are open, yet they see nothing of their many wild neighbors. Their ears, attuned to motorcars and traffic, seldom detect the music of Nature—the singing of birds, frogs, or crickets, or the wind in the leaves. These men, biologically illiterate, often fancy themselves well-informed, perhaps sophisticated. They know business trends or politics, yet haven't the faintest idea of what makes the natural world—the real world—tick."

Mr. Abraitys, in these brief essays, reaches out to those who live in megalopolis, and who may be unaware of the wilderness that is so close at hand. He reports what he has seen and although some of the accounts were written more than fifteen years ago, the subject matter is timeless.

Roger Tory Peterson

Preface

Within the complex and teeming confines of the great megalopolis which now stretches at least from Portland, Maine, to Richmond, Virginia, and among its industrial yards, its throughways and turnpikes, its airports and sprawling residential deserts lie thousands upon countless thousands of acres that are untouched and unknown.

To give comfort to the concerned environmentalist is the knowledge that there are more deer today, for instance, in this megalopolis than the red man ever dreamed of. It produces among its apparent wastes and forgotten corners more small mammals than ever. The rabbits, groundhogs, possums, skunks, and the like revel in the old fields, the junkyards, and disregarded wood lots and thickets. As we lost our forests our attendant emigrants (camp followers) moved in. The daisies of the field are new and the golden sheens of our roadsides are composed primarily of hieraciums, cinquefoils, and a host of others which are recent introductions from the far corners of the world.

In this megalopolis are still ponds untouched by habitations and less visited than in the time of the aborigines and swamps avoided. The bird watcher has found that the Carolina Wrens are moving north of the Mason-Dixon line. Red-bellied Woodpeckers are as common in the east today as were the Red-headed Woodpeckers of yesterday. The Mockingbird with the Turkey Vulture, Tufted Titmouse, and Cardinal, among others, are seen as far north as southern Canada.

This is a bit of the why of this book. Hopefully this is not a book of nay-saying, of weeping and deploring although much pessimism is natural in today's world. This book represents the pleasure, the joy and entertainment I have had in my environment, the wonder and awe and astonishment with which I have beheld the world about me and the desire to share these simple pleasures with my neighbors in my part of megalopolis.

For this book is composed of some of the articles which have been appearing in the *Hunterdon County Democrat* which is published in the county seat at Flemington, New Jersey. I began these articles back in the late 1950s. The careful reader may note that some of the material carries us a quarter of a century back in time. Here and there may be information which has since been changed or modified. Time has altered some of the bird ranges and some of the population counts. Some plants

PREFACE

have moved away, some plants have moved in. But then this is why we go into the field and this is why perhaps I get so many phone calls and letters from my neighbors. Each day is new and surprising.

The fact is a continual surprise to me, that so many people are interested. I was reared in this environment of Hunterdon County and a lonely and desolate environment it was in my childhood as the land was stripped in the 1920s of its farmers succumbing to the lure of the cities, as it struggled and bore through the wastes of the 1930s. I suppose I should look with caution on the land which has not treated me or my neighbors in the best of fashions. So many of those with whom I was reared say: "Why should I look at a warbler? Why should I be nice to a clump of weeds? What the hell did it ever do for me?"

But I was talking to a farmer in Warren County just this July of 1974. I was looking for Tuckerman's Carex, which is one of our state's lost plants, and this farm has some excellent wooded, calcareous swamps. He said, "You know, I was offered $400,000 for this cornfield over there last year and I refused it. It's got several hundred feet thickness of sugar sand on it, I think they called it, and some other good sand on it and they want to dig it out.

"I told them no. What good will the field be after that? I got this farm from my parents and I've got a son I want to leave it to. I want to leave it like I got it. As long as I can make a living off the cows it will stay the way it is."

Perhaps it is because there are still people like this farmer that I write this book. Perhaps it is because my neighbors will call me still to describe a bird they had never seen before and I catch the enthusiasm and joy and surprise in their voices as they describe the new. Perhaps it is because I can go out on a boat in the year of 1974 and within a mile of Atlantic City see a Wilson's Petrel pattering on the waves.

Maybe it is self-satisfaction, the pleasure of search and the satisfaction of discovery. I know it is partially to make a trip with a Scirpus expert like Ernie Schuyler and partake of his knowledge or listen to Lou Hand describe the acorns of all the oaks of New Jersey's Pine Barrens or share the enthusiasm of a Lee Edwards as we would batter our way through some humid and disagreeable swamp hip deep in mud and mosquito-bitten in search of some infinitesimally small plant which no one but ourselves, it seemed, cared about, or get sick on a small boat off the Hudson Canyon looking at shearwaters and hoping an albatross would come by. And perhaps it is a great deal more than that, things not known but merely sensed.

Certain decisions as to spelling and nomenclature have been made. As closely as possible works of a standard nature have been used, for in-

PREFACE

stance, the Eighth Edition of *Gray's Manual of Botany* and the Fifth Edition of the *A. O. U. Checklist of American Birds*, knowing full well that these, in part, are already in the process of change. Common or vernacular names are of the author's choice and those which are most descriptive were chosen. Bird names have been capitalized where a distinct species was denoted. The group name sparrow or sandpiper appears in lower case. Song Sparrow and Semipalmated Sandpiper are capitalized. I believe this makes for clearer understanding. If we write black rail do we mean a rail which was colored black and therefore unknown as to species or the Black Rail which defines our identification? This is applied to plants and animals, too. I will speak of a field of goldenrods but I will state the Seaside Goldenrod if I am speaking of that particular species.

An index of both vernacular and taxonomic names has been provided for the assistance of the reader. The literature on the subject of natural history has been expanded in recent years and guides of many kinds are available to the reader. A good library on the environment may be acquired quickly and economically by anyone interested in the world and the life around him.

The articles were written as they came to mind or as their incidents occurred. Many times I would go birding and end up checking out a swamp or go botanizing and become entranced by a frog along the way. Most of the trips in which I have led groups were done this way and seemed quite natural and accepted by everyone. The articles were not done as a task but as a spontaneous response to a subject at hand.

And I thank a host of people from Brower Hall in Florida to Ed Danforth in Maine, Joseph Muller, Floyd Wolfarth, Irving Black, and so many others whom I know and have known and who quite unconsciously assisted in writing this book.

Vincent Abraitys

I

The Backyard Wilderness

A Meadow

Along the little road runs a stone wall and beyond that was the meadow. The meadow was down in the bowl between these hills, and the wall ran beside its flatness. Across the narrow road the slope was immediate and on it was a hayfield.

The stone wall was old and untended and sprawled; very low and useless now as are all the old stone fences in the highlands of New Jersey and the big, rounded stones had spread to make a wide mounding.

As I stepped across it, a movement—a quick, brown movement at my feet—caught my eye and I froze. Here on the stones was a brown-patterned Milk Snake. Its coils were loosely arranged and a few inches of head and neck were buried in the stones.

I watched it. The snake's body would writhe and twist erratically. Then it would remain still awhile and only the heaving along the sides of its body would denote its exertion. It was oblivious of me.

The Milk Snake was shedding its skin. In time it would unwrap itself from the old, paper-thin outer scaling and in bright, new color it would return to the hayfield or the hillside.

I left the snake and stepped into this flat meadow between the hills. Just at its edge the meadow was still dry and the ground hard. At the stone wall were the dry plants, the Timothy and Wild Carrot, the Yarrow and Daisy, and the young plants of later goldenrod and aster.

There was a solid bed of Marsh Fern next, perhaps a foot high, and this marked the beginning of wetness. This would have marked the value of the meadow to the farmer, also, years ago when perhaps the cows roamed here. This was not a pasture of dry grasses fit for cows but a meadow of soggy wetness, poor for upland grazers, and the grayness of the Marsh Fern beds marked its beginning.

A meadow presents an uneven view to the eye from its edge. Its bed is flat but its growth is of uneven height. It has a few trees, a Sour Gum perhaps, or a cluster of Red Maple, or even a White Pine on a tiny hillock. Among the sprinkling of trees are scattered shrubs taller than a man. These would be alders and Poison Sumac, a chokeberry and Winterberry.

The local birds travel across the meadow, for it is only a small place among the hills. The vulture and the Red-tailed Hawk wheel over it, Blue Jays and Flickers fly across it. The Alder Flycatcher, singing its two-note sneeze, breeds in the meadow and the Yellow-throat Warbler, too. The "witchity-witchity" of the Yellow-throat is constant from the damp herbage. Wherever the cattails may be the Long-billed Marsh Wren hides its nest and here it sings its upside-down song.

A meadow has a stream. It may go through the center or it may be to one side. It will always be marked by a line of alders and willows and the Yellow Warbler will always be there as a scrap of yellow darting among the foliage.

The charm of the meadow is not in its birds or in the Milk Snake prowling its dry edges. Its charm and lure is in its plants, those plants that will not grow on dry land but demand that their roots be constantly in water. The meadow will be a wet world and all the plants will a be a new world of plants.

Beyond the Marsh Fern the St. John's-worts grow. These will not be the introduced European species that ranges our dry roadsides but coppery-yellow, big-petalled flowered ones hidden among the tussocks.

In early Summer the Burnet will bloom. It will grow high as a man's shoulder and wave thick wands of white flowers. Growing from among the Cinnamon Ferns it would appear as if the very ferns were blooming.

The eastern seaboard of our continent, given as it was to a solid deciduousness of forest, has few native grasses, but the meadows possess a bewildering series of scores of grass-resembling plants that classify as Carex, Juncus, Scirpus, Eleocharis, Rynchospora, and Cyperus.

Other than the technically-minded, few care to bother identifying these plants though numerous and fascinating they be. Most of them must be identified by their seeds, which may be seen clearly only under a lens, and this takes the edge off the fascination of the open, sunlit meadow. Perhaps the most evident of this grouping of plants is Carex stricta, which forms the tussocks of swamps and meadows along with the Juncus effusus. These tussocks are single clumps of colonies of this plant and they may form pedestal-like growths a foot wide and a foot above the wet soil. If one's balance is good they make excellent stepping points.

Should one part the plant growth at this spot to view the black, wet muck, another scene begins in the world of mosses and liverworts. The edge mosses here not yet in the center of the meadow are the wet mosses found everywhere. Only in the wettest center will one encounter the sphagnum species.

Growing with the true mosses is the dainty Meadow Spikemoss (Selaginella apoda). It is not a moss although it looks like one and grows like one. It is a close relative of the true ferns. Two of these curious spikemosses grow in New Jersey but each in an extreme habitat: Meadow Spikemoss creeps on the wet ground hidden from sun and wind; Rock Spikemoss sends evergreen tufts from between crevices of rocks high on our highest mountain ledges in the driest and windiest of habitats.

So with me you have crossed the stone fence at the road and have stepped into the meadow. Beyond the Sour Gum and over the narrow, alder-fringed stream on the far side is the upward sweep of the next hill. Past the Marsh Fern and standing next to the ruddy gracefulness of Poison Sumac the wetness of the meadow creeps in about the soles of our shoes. A small patch of bedstraw with white, minute blossoms is here and now in early July one yellow flower of the Marsh Cinquefoil has opened. A Cricket Frog leaps quickly into the safety of a tussock. The wet world is around us.

A Day in May

How fine it is that we do not easily outgrow the child's enchantment with clouds, for clouds are ever the substance of dreams, the reflected maps of far, unknown lands, the look of legendary places.

The dour skies of Winter, low and leaden, with their hurrying crows, have left us. Now in Spring we have this spilling, careless richness of creamy whiteness in huge meringues, horizon to horizon, an abundant, lush, and opulent froth upon the sky.

On a day in May, shortly after rain, when isolated masses of cumulus ripped from some distant source in the northwest ride singly over the zenith, comes the warbler time, and a horde of birds arrive, and the varieties of birds pass by.

The day is a welter and a tumult of song, a continual, melodious challenge from dawn to dusk and in the night, from a whirr of a Grasshopper Sparrow deep in the hayfields back of Ringoes to the Orchard Oriole singing atop the dying pear tree in Califon. And at midnight some Chat will awake to harass the Green Frog chorus.

Before the streets are filled the flutes of the Wood Thrush sound in the boroughs and in the damper woods the liquid precision of the Veery rises from the leaves like subterranean music. The vireos run their endless threads of song between the tree tops, webs of sound upon the air.

Undaunted by man with fierce and single purpose the birds make out the pattern of their year. The Catbird owns the Barberry bush without limitation, hard beside a busy railroad the Sora takes over the Flemington Junction marsh with a preoccupation only for other Sora. The Bobolink disdains the world for a scrap of molded grasses in a clump of weeds. Even the surly male Night Heron, duty bound, stands grumpily beside the nest, completely out of sorts, but duty bound.

All our resident warblers are with us in early May. The Teacher bird has gotten into all the scraps of woodlot and the Yellow Warblers at Sunnyside have picked such alders and viburnums as they need. Some hundreds of Redstarts have taken their favorite hanging grapevine in Hunterdon County from the seclusion of which they may see everyone, but in which no one sees them. This is the warbler secret. Brilliant as gem stones, fantastic in design, voluble in wonderful song, they have found the inner core of anonymity and the countless thousands go about unknown to me. Only the experienced ear and the patient eye can understand them.

Yellow-throats swarm in all our sedgy roadsides and the Chestnut-sided "wish to see Miss Beecher" are in every township. Kentucky Warblers do "poorly-poorly-poorly" near every rural bridge. We have the Cerulean lisping dreamily in the Sycamore tops along the Delaware and the Canada Warbler on the laurel hillsides of the Musconetcong. But only the young fox, wise at birth, knows them well. The young fox will hunt for mice.

Luckily for those held to lawns and gardens we have dozens of other species to substitute for these elusive wraiths, birds willing to recognize our vanity enough to live beside us. Robins will come to nest in the cherry trees and Barn Swallows in the wagon house. House Wrens share their happy, polygamous, polyandrous lives with us. Cardinals take up unfinal battles with convenient windowpanes. And the Baltimore Oriole, the painted blackbird of the operatic throat, reigns unchallenged over streets and towns.

In all the pleasant confusion of new sounds and new colors, the birds we have had about us during the Winter have dropped to the background. Who notices a Tufted Titmouse in May? But he is just as happy; he continues his prying about the shrubbery and indiscriminately scolds cat and squirrel, dog and man. With good sense avoiding the competition, his nest is set in some old woodpecker hole at some remote spot. His time will come again in December.

On the upper reaches of the South Branch near the Morris County line the Rose-breasted Grosbeaks are exceedingly common this early May. Singing males are spaced with regularity in the narrow valley, their voice a rich blend of the Scarlet Tanager's and Robin's song, but still retaining an individuality. The Louisiana Water Thrushes here have staked claims along the banks among the fishermen with no more conflict than with the Yellow-throated Vireos high in the elms.

Bartram's sandpiper, the Upland Plover, has returned to its traditional nesting field. Each year an anxiety runs among its friends, a fear that it will not return, but each year it manages to make the Patagonian round trip. A select few will hear its call.

Warbler time will soon pass but the residue will be in the Indigo Bunting's singing from a fence post, his blue camouflaged against June's sky, and in the Field Sparrow's sunny lay among the Black-eyed Susans. No one will worry about warblers in June, but this will not concern the warblers.

Parsleys

Golden Alexanders are out, the rich, creamy yellow of their bloom is scattered sparingly along damp wood's edge and roadside bank.

This is Zizia aurea, Zizia to honor Johann Baptist Ziz, a Rhenish botanist who lived from 1779 to 1829, and aurea from the Latin word for gold.

Most of the members of the parsley family, a large branch of plants, possess a dull white bloom not especially enticing to the eye. The family is easily recognized. All species have hollow stems and all produce a flat-topped flowering called an umbel, and the family name of Umbelliferae is derived from this fact.

The best plant from which to learn the parsleys is the well-known Queen Anne's Lace, or Wild Carrot, a species introduced from Europe which dominates waste places late in Summer. Golden Alexanders grow a foot or two high, possess a lustrous stem with smooth and firm dark green leaves, and umbels to a diameter of perhaps three inches. Generally, it is through blooming by the first of June.

This week in May perhaps gives us too much in yellows. Our eyes are too much dominated by the prevalent Yellow Rocket (Barbarea vulgaris) reaching over all grass and crop fields of the area. A bane to the farmer it may be, but at this time of year it has an appealing distinction to the eye in its yellow spreading over the roll of fields, so much a companion to the yellow of Dandelion at the roadbank.

But Yellow Rocket or River Rocket or River Salad is the pale yellow of the mustard family. It lacks the full gold of Alexanders, or the hues of Golden Ragwort, reminiscent of the sun-mad, delirious fantasy of the Van Gogh yellows.

Where the pastures are damp, where the fields dip to swales and stream banks, the perceptive eye quickly distinguishes the brilliant chrome of Senecio aureus, the Golden Ragwort, a name derived again from its color, senecio coming from the Latin *senex,* an old man, from the hoary look of some species. It has also been popularly called Groundsel or Squaw-weed.

Golden Ragwort is a small, slender plant and daisy-like in general appearance. It is a member of that disgustingly difficult group of plants called the Composites. But the sight of its gold blanket flung along our small, slow streams in May is identification enough.

The Shadbush white of April passes quickly to the evanescent white flowering of the Wild Plum, the heady fragrance too quick to pass, its tremendous perfume lingering only a few short days in too few spots. And then we have the Dogwood, lavish as always on our hillsides.

But another white flower is now blooming beneath the Dogwood, a small parsley, the Sweet Cicely.

To help those who wish to identify this plant, it should be pointed out that there is another plant just as abundant as Sweet Cicely and scarcely distinguishable from it. This is the Anise Root.

Neither of these plants are striking in their small clusters of dull cream flowers, but their leaves and stem have a wonderful odor of anise when they are bruised. Both produce roots that are edible, that of the Anise Root being spicier, but in the interests of safety this plant could be confused with Poison Hemlock and therefore should not be tampered with by beginners. Merely test the stem and leaves for their aroma.

While on the parsleys I can add another that is easily found by everyone. This is the Cow Parsnip, a huge, ungainly herb with a hollow stem that grows up to eight feet high and with large, deeply cut leaves. It is rampant now in the South Branch Valley and in the valley of the Delaware, but will not bloom until June.

If you are near a wettish spot, you will encounter the Spring Cress in full flower. This is one of the mustard group not particularly beautiful but its four-petalled whiteness as it grows in groups contrasts with the long-stemmed beauty of the Marsh Violets. These pale blue violets with deep purple centers are now at climax. Like most of our showier flowers they use a habitat most people shun, to their own loss.

The Sweet Vernal Grass is now at its peak. Bruised beneath the cattle's hooves, the pasture cows walk in its perfume on the red shales of the Amwell Valley, and already running through the grass is the early blooming Bulbous Buttercup. Green is May, true, and fragrant, but it is a month of golden flowering.

The Phoebe

A phoebe came through on the afternoon of March 16th. This was the first bird of the year, neither very early nor very late for it is anytime in March that the first of this species is seen although it is April that brings the abundance.

It was late in the afternoon and the day was bright, chilly, and whippy, the wind blowing so that the phoebe, when he came, flew low to the ground.

First he alit on the lowermost branch of a pear tree where I first identified him, the small, dark bird unobtrusive on the bough. His demeanor befitted a new season, trim and neat. He looked about the near air confident and alert, the dark eyes glistening with life.

Next he moved to a Rose of Sharon bush where, as he settled, he vigorously flitted his tail up and down which is so characteristic of every phoebe. Shortly, and still moving close to the ground, he flew toward an Arrow-wood shrub where in his path he encountered the eddy of wind about the corner of a building and this drove him almost to the dry grass of the field.

The wind was a torment to him here in the open. It blew the feathers on his flanks askew so that when he gained the Arrow-wood twig he twitched his body to adjust the ruffled down.

Here, too, he searched the wind for a possible insect but the March gale held none and with a final flick of his tail he made his determined flight a yard above the ground for the distant fence-line trees, a purposeful mote of life confident and sure in Spring.

The flycatchers are not singers, nor are they gaudy of wing, and many are the bird students who ignore them. But I am partial to them. I am partial to phoebes. This quiet bird of quiet ways is agreeable to me. His is the voice of silent farmyards at dawn and the manner of cool glens near country bridges at dusk.

There was a phoebe I knew once, years ago, who built annually on our porch. A nest green with mosses on a porch rafter was all we knew of him except for the throaty phoebe calls in the early morning.

While the Robins squealed hysterically and the Catbird was raucous, while the House Wren tore his throat with singing and the Song Sparrows battled viciously for their nest sites, the phoebe went his quiet way, only the nervous flick of tail showing the intense concern it had for the young in the moss and brown nest.

The Baltimore Oriole could be blatant in the afternoon and the Barn Swallows could dive at the barn cat screaming raw invectives and the Chippy male sing all the wonderful day but the phoebe limited himself to a buzzy, throaty greeting of the dawn and thereafter studiously attended to his family's wants, not deterred by the June sun or the exuberance of June or the windmill tilting of the flashy, boisterous males of other species.

The birds nested a number of years but then came a Spring when no nest was built. Only one phoebe had returned to the family site. It was the male. Each morning he flew to the wire near the house. Next he moved to a stub of the hickory high over the lane. Finally he would go to the old weather-vane on the garage.

At each place he vigorously and lustily called the two note "fee bee" proclaiming that here was a good territory and he had staked it out and was ready for a mate.

He caught flies in the open air and he sang. He did this all day through the weeks of May and far into June but no female came that year.

Then he disappeared and no phoebe has used that porch rafter since.

Of course I have seen phoebes since. One cannot live in Hunterdon County without seeing phoebes. I have found them on all the bridges of the rural roads where they make their nests on the girders beneath the traffic, oblivious of the noise a foot above their heads.

I have seen them along woodland streams perkily flitting their tails, and along the dirt roads the traveler is never too far from the soft throaty call.

On the cliffs we find their nests. Here were their sole nesting areas before porch rafters and bridges and they are still used. The nest is put on a little ledge below a larger one so the driving rain does not reach it.

The phoebes sail out from the rock walls to snip unwary insects from the air or they perch on the barkstripped limb of dead trees as dark spots against the lighted sky. Their soft, fuzzy cries echo from the cliffs.

Perhaps the phoebes are overlooked. Most often they are ignored. But the chance is that no vainglory possesses the bird and he accepts the inattention as the peace of the woodland stream and the dusted pool beneath the bridge.

The little bird is dark. The eye is black and the bill is black and his lightest feathers are a sooty brown. But his is the black and dark of the

Phoebe

smaller beings of the wild, the innocent, the black and dark of protection, of shadow and fay.

Guileless and demure the sober-cloaked bird comes in March and departs in October and for all his whispering "fee bee," his mark is as gentle as a falling leaf. Withal he returns, for the world has a place for him. I am partial to the phoebe.

At the Portals of June

The end of May is still unseemingly chilly and many of May's early flowerings still display their beauty at the portals of June.

But these days, for all their chill, have been glorious, airy and perfumed, bright, and the wind as soft as apple blossoms falling.

Now in the last week of May the Blackpoll Warblers are moving through the wood and their notes out of the treetops are like tinkling silver coins. The Blackpoll Warbler is a late awakener to Spring. He is the last of those sprites called the wood warblers to go northward to his nesting grounds.

I do not know why they are one of the latest of movers to the north. Perhaps the thick shade of the balsam and the spruce still holds Winter's ice atop New England's higher peaks and that inclemency holds them with us long after the first of the Robins have left their nests in New Jersey.

Much as the song of Bobolinks can hold us spellbound through May, it is the magnificent coloring of these days that is a marvel to the eye and more constant than song. The eyes are Winter-starved for color and May fulfills the hunger in rampant waves of white and yellow. It is plum and cherry blossom, apple and viburnum.

The Orchard Oriole is wild with song in the tulip trees but just as satisfying are the buttercups and rockets, violets and daisies. The golden senecios are an ache in the heart. Once more the Mandrake, or May Apple, blooms on the forest floor far beneath the little chorus of Blackpoll Warblers. It has the sweetest of perfumes, appley and winey, intoxicating and unforgettable. What a wonderful world for the forest creatures is this time of year, this season of cidery perfume!

As I went to gather hawthorn blossoms I heard the Indigo male on his song that ran on and on in seeming endlessness. Here in the east only the long song of the Winter Wren approaches the length of the Indigo Bunting's song.

The hawthorn blossoms were a blanket of white, a sheet tossed on thorny branches. But they had a rank, ammonia odor about them, strong and almost unpleasant. I noticed that the Mountain Ashes have this odor about them so that it may be a characteristic of some branches of the Rose family.

The hawthorns, Crataegus, are a widespread family of thorny shrubs. They could not be called abundant in number but they seem to be everywhere. Unfortunately, so few people know them except in derogatory language.

I was taking hawthorn blossoms and the first of the leaves to label and save. In September I hopefully will go to the same sites and gather the reddish fruits for samples. Then with both fruits and flowers and leaves perhaps I will be able to identify the various species that grow in Hunterdon County. They are a tough genus to understand.

I did recognize with ease one of our species but, alas, it was an introduced species. This is the English Hawthorn which is scattered east of Copper Hill towards Reaville as I found it, although it may be at other spots, too.

But if I never untangle the riddles of the Crataegus family I will be just as satisfied with the splendid sight of these thorny shrubs in blossom and I will never forget the strong stench of the flowers.

Warblers

About the time the Pinxter Flower opens in our woodlands, but before the catkins have dropped from the White Oaks, the warblers pass through Hunterdon County on their way north.

Thirty-nine species of this family have been recorded from Hunterdon, but the casual observer sees few, so nervous and so small are they, and their passage so swift. Actually, a number of them begin moving up in April. These include the Orange-crowned, the Pine, and both Palm Warblers. By the end of April each rocky woodland brook has a pair of Louisiana Water Thrushes every few hundred yards, their piping song known only to the trout fishermen. And every farm wood lot, no matter how humble, has Thoreau's little Golden-crowned Thrush, the Ovenbird, singing "teacher-teacher-teacher" in the evenings.

But most of us know the warblers as bright scraps of color flashing

THE BACKYARD WILDERNESS

in the apple trees, disturbing the bees among the apple blossoms, or like golden beetles whirring in the new leaves of the hickories. The entire family is noted for its striking coloration pattern. Here is the Blackburnian of the flaming orange throat; the Redstart, scarlet and jet, Candelita of the Caribbean; the Mourning with its sorrowing gray-black; the golden Prothonotary. Nothing can be bluer than a Cerulean in sunlight, nor greener than a Nashville's mantle.

Ornithologists early ran out of descriptive names for them and resorted to mere tagging: Chestnut-sided, Black-throated Green, Bay-breasted, Black-throated Blue. Or called them Cape May or Kentucky or Canada from the locale where first seen. Or, as with the Myrtle, derived a name from its habit of feeding on the Bayberry along the coastal beaches in Winter.

Ordinarily the warblers will hit us in a bewildering swarm on hot May mornings, but not so this year. And the reports from the Philadelphia and New York areas and in between are in the form of a question: Where are the warblers? Recent reports from all over the country contain only a few warblers and these mostly our resident Chats, Yellow-throats, Blue-wings, and Black-and-whites. However, a closer scrutiny going back into April shows listings of virtually all species with some rarer types included, such as the Hooded, Lawrence's, Wilson's, and Tennessee.

Perhaps we have a clue in the action of the Blackpoll Warbler. It may well be that some of the heat waves of late April and early May shot our warblers far to the north of us, and long before we expected them.

Birds in general are in good supply. Even birds in the semi-rare group like the Orchard Oriole, Scarlet Tanager, Least Flycatcher, Warbling Vireo, and Rose-breasted Grosbeak are abundant this year. Certainly all our common breeding warblers are here. The rare ones are in, too. The Yellow-throated came in on April 30th, and the Ceruleans are singing as usual high in the trees of the Delaware Valley. The Kentuckys are not at all uncommon in the deeper woods. In the meantime, all good birders will await the Fall migration.

Color in Mid-Summer

Chicory is blue now on the roadsides and Queen Anne's Lace is over all the fields. Bouncing Bet is flowering and the Joe-pye-weeds are beginning to open.

VINCENT ABRAITYS

During the humid phases of mid-summer we are apt to pass not seeing these marvelous splashes of color along our normal ways. Yet the flowers are there. Along the canal that runs beside the highway from Raven Rock to Trenton the season's finest display is starting to unfold. This is the explosion of Purple Loosestrife that has found a friendly haven on the wet banks of the waterway.

Not that Purple Loosestrife is confined to here alone. It is partial to any spot that will wet its feet. It is on all the gravel bars of the Delaware. It is also on the shores of the river and it is solid masses on the low-lying islands. It is also in the South Branch Valley and various others. It follows up all the tributaries where among the wet it can find a little sun.

But along the canal the traveler is deliciously assailed with mile after mile of purple blooming, tall on the damp banks, bee-laden and odorous among the yellow goldenrods and sunflowers.

Lythrum Salicaria is a comparatively recent immigrant to our continent but like all of us who are comparatively recent newcomers to this continent it has done very well for itself.

Today if one wishes to study our original flora one must go to the woodlands. To such areas has it retired.

Our old vegetation predominates in its original habitat of marsh and stream bank in the shade, swamp and sterile mountaintop, and throughout our forests. Here it can withstand the competitive onslaught of the immigrants and in this habitat it has fared better than its companion inhabitants, the aboriginal Indians, have fared against us.

Were you to go out on the roadsides and fields, the old lawns and waste places to catalogue the flowers, you would find that fully nine out of ten of the herbs and plants we know so well are introductions from other lands. Like all of us they have come to these shores within the last few hundred years.

If one will bear in mind that our eastern seaboard was once a forest predominantly consisting of plants adapted to forest conditions it is easy to understand why these weeds have become so well established.

For after our forests were cut our continent had no grasses, no herbs, no shrubs that could tolerate the open, drying conditions of tree-less earth. Such conditions had never existed here and no plant was ready to take over this openness.

But on the European continent that had been open and cultivated for hundreds, thousands of years there had evolved a vegetation suitable to an open, windy, drying sunny life and this vegetation came with us and, like us, it has taken over and dominated this continent.

The plants of Europe were honored and honorable. Not only did they delight the eye and pacify the sense but they served the people. They were in the daily life of the people, in their folklore and their history, and they were known more thoroughly than any plant is known today.

They were called herbs and worts, mints and sallats. They were potherbs, greens, and teas to suit the palate, to soothe, please, and minister to the mind and body.

There were officinals and medicinals, lotions and potions suitable for coughs and the pox and all manner of ailments. Modern medicine is grounded in the old apothecary shops of history.

Time has passed them by. Their glorious history has languished, their old reputes are forgotten today. Today they are weeds—but let us add that they are honorable weeds.

And let us not forget that Chicory is of the heavenly hue and the Black-eyed Susans are always a rich gold and the Purple Loosestrife in late Summer is a pretty sight along the banks of the Delaware and Raritan Canal.

Hot Days

There is little of incentive in the dreary days of August when the humidity dulls the senses and the heat enervates the very soul.

On some late afternoons towards the still and sticky evening a distant spectacle appears on the horizon. Late thunder clouds appear of a dangerous and awesome yet spectacular pink in the distance.

The clouds pile on, an intricate fleecing of pink and white, a sculptured pillowing that changes continually, but always remains the same. At this distance great storms have more beauty than danger in the beholding.

But these storms bring no relief, no dry and cooling winds. If they persist after the sun goes down they show a dazzling display of lights and flashes for a time and then they dwindle into the horizon.

All animal life remains sensibly quiet in the extraordinary heat. At midday nothing moves except perhaps the swallows coursing the cool sky or the Chimney Swifts. Even my groundhog remains underground in the cool earth.

Only a pair of House Wrens are busy. They had a late brood. They got them off the nest only last week. Now they are chattering and talking in the hot morning as they coach and cajole the youngsters along the way to self sufficiency. They stay close in the burdock denseness, feeding down in the safeness of a blackberry thicket. In this crisis they must ignore the heat.

Toward evening activity resumes. A pair of fawns comes out to feed in the field. They are half grown and still full of curiosity, not with an adult's suspicion, and I can toll them in. But they lose interest in the game and with a flick of white tails they move into the next field.

The fawns are not careful yet. They come out too early but they learn from watching the adults who wait until almost darkness before they slip out of the Black Haws to graze in the fields.

But to a young deer the day is still too long and so they come out early to assuage the hunger pangs. They have patience and fortitude yet to learn.

The young House Wrens learn all these things quickly and easily and in a few days the adults will not need to chatter and the entire family will disperse through the asters and the goldenrods.

But color to please the eye is rich on the roadsides. It has been a long time since Queen Anne's Lace has put on such a display. Some road banks and many fields have been a billowy white with it.

If you wish you may call this the Wild Carrot and if you are disposed to taste things you may gather some of the roots for eating. However the roots are tiny things and stringy.

Two friends have commented on the Rose Pink profusion of this year. This plant, Sabatia angularis, is one of the few inland species of this genus. It is appealing to the eye and would need no further work for even a sophisticated gardener.

This member of the gentian family grows on dry, undisturbed hillsides preferably. It moves in about the time the early goldenrods get in or the Beard Grass or Indian Grass and it stays until the Bayberry comes and the Red Cedar and Dogwood begin to choke the smaller growths.

Equally and perhaps more flamboyant is the Blazing Star, which is beginning to bloom around the county. This single-stem plant has purple heads in a row at the tip and narrow, linear leaves. It is no more common either than the Rose Pink and neither plant should ever be picked because of its rarity.

Plants of this sort are transient in a habitat. They come into those fields where plowing has stopped and where a sod has been stabilized. They move in with many other plants and they disappear as a forest canopy develops.

Locations for these species, therefore, are not constant although I know of some roadside banks which have stabilized as to plant life and the Blazing Star and Rose Pink appear there annually. They will remain there so long as the banks are not changed.

Now then, while it is too hot to go looking for birds it is a good time to look at our wild flowers. All you need do is drive down any little-used road to gorge on Summer color.

Horned Larks

In Summer, a bird the color of dust will start from the dust of the roadside. Or the bird may rise from the sparse stubble of open fields in Spring. The small brown bird will flutter away and be lost quickly upon the brownness of the landscape. Thus will the Horned Lark be encountered.

The Prairie Horned Lark that breeds in New Jersey is closely related to the Skylark of the Old World. Its size and habits are similar and what it lacks in song from its European relative it makes up in attractiveness, for it is much more colorful.

In Spring, like the Skylark, it ascends high in the air and at this height it begins a slow, downward spiral, singing all the while. It is his declaration that a bit of stubble field or barren roadside is his and his alone and upon it his young shall be reared.

Our Horned Lark breeds early. True, some young will be seen in June but April is their nesting month and some pairs begin breeding early in March.

Few people are aware of breeding Horned Larks. But where their specific demands are satisfied—on the treeless flat and open fields shorn of grasses or the barrens outcropped in gravel and sand—it is a plentiful bird.

Mostly it is the farmer out on early Spring plowing who perceives the Horned Lark but usually bird and farmer are equally busy and neither concerns itself with the other. The youngsters drowsily walking to school down the wide dirt roads of morning will occasionally flush the bird out but April and May are so full of Spring's marvels that a single bird is rarely noted.

The Horned Lark is agreeable to his situation. He is not a lonely bird. He is gay and joyous. His companions are the wind and the strong sunlight of April. He eschews the thicket. Bud and leaf of tree are not for him, his is the wide and running emptinesses.

VINCENT ABRAITYS

In Winter the little larks assemble. The brown birds gather in large flocks. They dance over the fields on constant discovery.

When snow is on the ground with its whiteness everywhere the Horned Larks become evident. The brown birds in flocks of ten to several hundred may be seen walking on the snow to gather the windblown seeds.

Always seed eaters, the deepest snows never diminish their food supply for the wind will always blow and no snow is so high that it will cover the tops of all the weeds. They are nourished in the most frigid weather and their songs tinkle all the more gaily as they fly the faster on the wind.

In these seasons they are joined by even more northern visitors; Redpolls may be close by and Snow Buntings who come from as far as Greenland.

The secretive Longspur from the plains and tundra of Saskatchewan for lack of flocks of his own will join the larks and creep inconspicuously among them. If the Horned Larks are hard to see, the Longspur will be even more difficult. But he will be somewhere in any large Horned Lark flock upon the snow.

Our Prairie Horned Lark sports two tiny ear tufts from which he takes his name. Beneath a yellowish throat he has a narrow band of black. Another narrow band of black also curves, down beneath his eye.

The Northern Horned Larks as a subspecies mingle freely with the Prairies. They have no differences, but around the first of March they recognize their kind and their destiny and quietly leave our fields for the northward journey.

One other race of larks may be found in New Jersey, the Hoyt's. Hoyt's breed westward of the Northern Larks in high central Canada and therefore tend to winter more in the central areas of the United States. Now and then single Hoyt's are found in the northeastern United States with other larks. Actually, the Hoyt is no more than a large Prairie Horned Lark with a somewhat darker back. It is distinguished as a subspecies because of this small difference and that it remains geographically distinct on its own breeding grounds.

These then are the three races of Horned Larks which occur in New Jersey. These three are among the 21 races which are listed for North America north of Mexico.

But the larks are more than entities in museum displays. They are wisps of wind and straws of sunlight and a whisper of song across the heating fields of March. They make the old stubbles proud and give reason to the sterile gravels. They make alive the back fields far from the roads.

Ashes and Hickories

In Prallsville at Smiths' Mill along the road are a number of gigantic ash trees, big as any that I have seen around. He who planted them years ago possessed vision.

The ash is a tree that is common enough in this area but while there are a number of kinds of ash the stands through here run almost solid to the White Ash. Finding another species is generally accidental and always a matter of habitat.

The names of the kinds of ash run to color. There is the White, the Red, the Green, the Black. Years ago botanists recognized many species of ash but today the thinking allows but four species in our state.

Now and then among the White Ash stands is found a variety that is heavily velvety as to leaves. This is not thought to be a different tree but is classed as the Biltmore. It is found sporadically through our area.

I do not recall seeing the Red Ash in Hunterdon County but I have encountered it in Warren County. It is a typical swamp tree and I suppose a search would disclose its presence in Hunterdon.

The Green Ash is another rare ash and one that is difficult to identify. It can be encountered in the Delaware River Valley where it grows on the sandy, wetter flats on and near the banks. Periodic flooding does not injure it.

The Black Ash also likes wet feet. It is found in the wettest sections of swamps where water is likely to remain about its roots for the entire year. Its companions are the alder and the Poison Sumac.

The Black Ash is found in Hunterdon County as a small, gnarled tree of wooded swamps. Like the Red and Green, the Black must be classed as rare. In fact, I have seen Poison Sumac at more spots than I have seen Black Ash. I think the count on the spots for Poison Sumac is now up to five, all of them being in our northern hills, luckily in spots where people are unlikely to encounter it.

But as to the ash trees of Hunterdon, for all general purposes they may be called White Ash with little fear of error in identification.

The hickories are a bit different. All of the species of hickories are widespread compared to the ash family and care ought to be used in naming them.

VINCENT ABRAITYS

By far the easiest to identify is the Shagbark. This is the hickory that years ago was allowed to grow and even encouraged for the sake of its heavy and delicious nut crop. No one but the squirrel harvests the crop today but the big trees with their platey, peeling bark remain on the fence lines and along the roadsides.

The Mockernut, or White-heart Hickory, is abundant on our wooded hillsides. It is a good timber hickory and it also has sweet kernels, but, alas, the kernel is encased in a thick, hard shell and that is why the early Dutch called it the Moker-noot, or Heavy-hammer Nut.

There are two species of Pignut that grow through here but they are exceedingly difficult to separate in the field. The Small Pignut as opposed to the Pignut tends to have a bark that is eventually scaley. The fruit is rounder than the oval fruits of the Pignut and the husk splits freely to the base, not half-way as in the Pignut. While these differences are stable, perhaps one is merely a variety of the other.

The Bitternut Hickory is found in Hunterdon, too, but it is the least frequent, being downright scarce. It has nine small leaflets whereas our more abundant species run from five to seven. There are a few trees along Alexauken Creek and along the Delaware between Stockton and Raven Rock. There are doubtless other stations.

A tree that intrigues me is the Shellbark Hickory, or Big Shagbark or King Nut. It is a westerly tree that has enormous fruits with sweet kernels. It is reputed to grow here and there in Bucks County in Pennsylvania and I see no reason why it cannot be found in Hunterdon County, certainly in the Delaware drainage. A search ought to be made for it.

Only one other hickory grows in New Jersey. This is the Pale Hickory which is a southern tree that enters our state along the lower coastal plain. Several years ago I endeavored to locate a specimen of the Pale Hickory for my own satisfaction. I had found that even our southern Jersey naturalists knew little of it.

I located my first specimen off Route 47 near Rio Grande in lower Cape May County. After studying this, finding other trees was simple. With the help of a few other plant enthusiasts we were able to determine that it was a fairly widespread tree in Cape May and Cumberland Counties.

The Hackberry is not known to be a large tree except in the Delaware drainage or, more properly, in the valley itself. There was a monster of a Hackberry growing on the banks of the Lockatong where it empties into the canal near Raven Rock but the flood of 1955 ripped out this tree. It compared with any oak or sycamore for girth and height.

Shagbark

THE BACKYARD WILDERNESS

I have found another giant Hackberry. This one stands on the banks of the Delaware in Riegelsville where the Musconetcong enters the river. It's a big brute of a tree and sometime I ought to measure it. It might go for a record.

Searching for Unusual Plants

In a column I wrote in 1959 I referred to the discovery by two of my botanist friends living in southern New Jersey of a hitherto undescribed species of Utricularia in a sand pond off in a obscure section of Atlantic County.

Utricularias are commonly called bladderworts, and are plants that grow in water. They are equipped with hollow traps upon their roots which are actually leaves and branches growing underground or beneath the surface of the water. These traps, or bladders, are able to ensnare underwater animal life which serve to partially nourish the plant.

This particular bladderwort was not known by the professional botanists consulted and its description was not listed in either Gray or Fernald. Further research, however, has determined this is a tropical plant which does occur in Seminole County, Florida. How it got to New Jersey no one knows.

While I am sad for my friends that they have missed the opportunity to describe a new species and to attach their names to it, it does not detract from the brilliance of their botanical coup inasmuch as neither are professionals. In fact, both are plumbers by trade.

Those of us who prowl the nooks and corners of this state continually come upon the new, the unexpected. Occasionally we come upon old things which are new to us. This happened to me recently.

I was in Warren County with a fellow plant searcher on the trail of a truly rare and obscure rush reputed to have grown at one time near a single pond. We did find this Nut Rush, but what intrigued me most at the site on which the Grass of Parnassus and the Fringed Gentian also were growing profusely was the bog muck and the pond bottom. It was pure white.

This soil was the whiteness of chalk and the fineness of high-grade pulverized limestone, and in little windrows here and there were countless shells, snail shells of various kinds, mostly broken, but some absolutely perfect.

Therefore I consulted that good authority on things geological, Edward Arnitz of Quakertown, for an explanation of this odd situation and Ed supplied me with the proper information.

He tells me there are many spots in northwestern Jersey where there are beds of this shell marl composed of shells and shell material and fresh water mollusks, the gastropods being most numerous.

This is a comparatively recent formation and present-day snails are continually adding their tiny bit to the old accumulation. Here and there these beds have piled up to a depth of 14 feet and at one time they were worked commercially. Today the beds are undisturbed.

This marl is found only in situations favorable to the snail, in watery areas, in marshes, and in poorly drained depressions. In many places vegetation has overgrown the marl and it is then found at various depths beneath the peat and soil. It also is constituent of many lake beds. Later in the day we came upon an old sink hole which now is dry and the marl was present there.

This process is directly concerned with the last glacial stage of the Pleistocene wherein many lakes and ponds were left after the ice retreat from the limestone sections of Warren and Sussex Counties. Certainly many of these beds were formed since then only to be completely eroded away. Yet enough of them remain to be of intense interest to the ecologist and geologist.

In this vein I recently came into possession of sections of fossilized cypress from down near Gibbsboro in Camden County. It is buff in color, completely stony, and came out of the Kirkwood formation, a not very old formation back in the Miocene.

It is sometimes difficult to understand why with so many strange and wonderful things so close to home, so many of which are unexplained, so many of which remain to be discovered, man persists in trying to colonize the moon.

Birds of Winter

The Winter birds now have settled down to a comfortable routine. All birds that are migratory have left and the northern birds who share our weather have arrived to supplement those species who stay with us regardless of the season.

Two fields away in an old pasture of cedar and Black Haw overrun

THE BACKYARD WILDERNESS

with grape, honeysuckle, and bittersweet vine, they have spent the night secure from wind and fox and cat. In the dark morning of the short December days they trickle out to the stubble of a grass field. Here they creep about to glean what the diligent mice have left.

The flock is never still and their travel next is up a fence line which runs besides a ditch, and then they will cross the road to pass around the house. By this time the sun is up and the first birds to be seen in the group will be the Cardinal and the Blue Jay, their colors flashing in the cherry tree. The Blue Jay will be silent, but the Cardinal will be giving his alarm note a hundred yards away.

The first birds to reach the house, however, will be the chickadees who are always eager to arrive, but the first to leave. They will launch themselves from the ragged milkweeds across the road to the twigs of the apple trees in the yard, making small sounds of conversation to each other all the while. The chickadees are the acknowledged leaders of the Winter birds. They seek the way, and all the others follow.

Against the ground, beneath the chickadees, come the juncos, flashing their white tail feathers in erratic play. They keep up a constant chatter on the frozen ground, exclaiming in glee over each tiny bit of seed. A few Song Sparrows are attracted by the clamor, but finding little to interest them they return to the roadside shrubs.

Along the flanks of the flock where the Cardinal calls his alarm at nothing, the timid White-throats scratch unseen among the leaves. The bolder Tree Sparrows betray their presence by continually flitting among them.

As the flock passes onward the Goldfinches appear, now feeding on the ground, now joining the Jay in the treetop. Finally, in restless boredom they wing for the high trees of the woodlot. A Downy Woodpecker just out of his bed in the maple branch sleep-drowsy wanders undecidedly through the flock, then flies ahead to look for borers in the downed stalks of a cornfield.

Soon the flock is gone for the day, off to the wood and fields down the hollow. Sometime in late afternoon they will be heard as they chatter and bicker themselves homeward to the dark cedars of the old pasture field.

The days are more exciting around feed stations where the birds may be viewed from the comfort of warmed rooms. Here and there a towhee braves out the Winter, and perhaps an oriole or Brown Thrasher. Mockingbirds now have become a staple.

Purple Finches are everywhere and House Finches have arrived. The latter are western birds which recently have taken root in the east. All Purple Finch flocks should be checked carefully for these new birds since they are quite similar. They do lack the eye stripe and their color is not as deep as the Purple Finch, and they do not possess the tail notch. Now and then House Finches will travel with English Sparrows.

Evening Grosbeaks, thick-billed, yellow birds of sedate carriage, have been reported now from just about all areas. Pine Siskins have appeared at various spots, and the first Redpolls of the season have been spied.

Near Center Bridge over in Solebury Township, a western visitor, the Ash-throated Flycatcher, made a surprise appearance on December 2nd. This bird has never been reported previously in the Commonwealth of Pennsylvania, or for that matter on the eastern seaboard.

Dave Johnson first saw the bird and sent word on to me. Shortly after I located it, Alan Brady of the Delaware Valley Ornithological Club came up from Newtown and both of us studied this strange wanderer. The next day and for several days afterward numerous birders from the Philadelphia area combed the vicinity but the bird had gone. Thus is the routine of our usual days enlivened by the visit for a day of a small continental traveler.

The Shibboleths of Autumn

The shibboleths of Autumn are many; the falling leaf and the fallen petal, the aster's dry rustling and the frost-hollow morns. The red leaf falls and the dark bones of tree grasp an empty sky.

Certainly the Autumns are not for singing, not for June's riotous song, and the somber dress of juncos befits the lowering year. The muted twittering of juncos dressed in gray is song enough for October.

And the gaudy jay, nervous and impelled, hysterically roves the casting boughs and the Red Squirrel nervously scolds in the grape vine. Bird and animal proceed with the age-old rituals of Winter preparation.

Now the groundhog lays by his store of fat and the Gray Squirrels in angry irritation patter firm the well-hidden walnuts. Late moths seek out their hiding places for the Winter.

The Red Fox is joyous. Now he lives in the world. He can forget the panting-hot days of August when he sweltered in the thicket, when he dug deeply between the tree roots for the cooling dampness of dirt.

Remember July of sultry quietude? Then time hung suspended over the daisy fields. Higher then was the sun.

THE BACKYARD WILDERNESS

The sun is fallen now, the July has gone. The fox is rampant on the hills. The small, fast feet running are silent in the frost-jeweled grass and the merest of air movements alone betrays their rapid passing.

Autumn is the last cry of bird, the sadness of a fallen leaf.

Autumn is a light upon the hills. On the afternoons of October the colors rage upon the hills.

On Sandy Ridge and Fisher's Peak the oaks and tulips glory. Across Fuchsenberg and Schooley's Mountain and clear to Gravel Hill the colors run. The Musconetcong is aflame.

Yet, incontrovertibly, the red leaf loosens from its socket upon the twig. Inexorably the red leaf severs and falls. The year goes down.

The hawks in hungry circles cross the sky. Beneath them in the swaths of Summer grass, dry and accumulated, are the hordes of vole and lemming, of mouse and shrew.

Summer's accumulation will dwindle. As the Summer's grass is ingested in the myriad stomachs so the Summer's horde of rodents will succumb to the hungry circles in the sky.

And as the daylight lessens and the hawks move southward, as the nights increase and the sun goes southward throughout the dark hours the northern owls shall come and in the long nights the hungry owls will prey over Summer's accumulation of grasses. Under the impact mole, rat, vole, lemming, and shrew will dwindle and earth's balance shall return as Spring.

But October is the night of the deer on the hawthorn hills, night of the ambling, dawdling coon rustling the corn-heavy stalks.

Ah, but these fantastic nights when the stars are hard and glittering and the wind rolls by! It is the north wind.

The north wind in the night of October is the sound of April and old dreams, it is a confirmation of sharp-tanged memory and late birds flying. It is a confusion of apples and petals.

Despite all Indian Summer when the breeze in mid-afternoon is a smiling memory of old pleasures there is the sharp knifing that Autumn is a time of the bird's last cry.

October is the leaf falling. October is the fallen petal.

Murder in the Air

For a time it appeared as if mayhem would be done on a Mockingbird here at my home. That is what my wife threatened as a minimum.

VINCENT ABRAITYS

The Mocker decided to sleep in a small spruce outside our bedroom window. The word sleep is not correct actually. He spent the night in the spruce but he did not sleep at all. He sang hour after hour, monotonously and without let up.

Now, a Mocker has little of his own song. He imitates the calls and songs of other birds and he has a tremendous repertoire. The listener is not lulled by a dreamy, continuous melody like the repetitiveness of the Wood Thrush lay at dusk. He is subjected to a jarring and jumpy conglomeration of sounds.

To try to sleep some eight yards from a Mocker going full blast on phoebe, Blue Jay, meadowlark, and a dozen other hi-fi songs is almost impossible. The sound is too loud and the ears never know what is coming next.

I think this Mocker has had an uneven love life this Spring. In April, he acquired a mate and things appeared to be going well. Much mutual devotion was displayed. Then, for reasons I have not been able to fathom, an incompatibility set in and all day the pair did nothing but brawl. Nothing went right. I do not know who was to blame, but at last the female departed.

That is when this business of singing all night began. To have lost a mate did not lessen my Mocker's ego. He promptly launched a round-the-clock advertising campaign.

I will say he did a good job. When he slept or when he ate I do not know, but I do know he was calling the high heavens that he was available and my wife and I thereby became the prime sufferers.

During the day he perched on the chimney and would pause only to glare at me whenever I stepped outside the door. I did not like this because I had nothing to do with his problems. During the nights he did not pause at all.

It paid off for him. He got a new mate and things have quieted down. For this situation I am thankful. The other female was kind of a brassy affair, not at all afraid of people. The present one is a timid sort who flies off the minute the door is opened.

But she is maternally minded. She has been picking up small sticks and grass stems and has been carrying them here and there. It does not seem yet that she has come to the decision as to where she will build, but she is looking.

I hope she stays. He has stopped glaring at me and is holding his song at a reasonable level. I hope he keeps it that way.

II

Some Basics

Thoughts on Bird Calls and Formation Flying

A flight of geese went to the northward the other evening. One knew they were there in the dark sky by the throaty honk-honk drifting down.

Why do geese call in the sky? Why do they advertise their presence? Geese, adult geese, have no enemies in the sky at night but the small birds flying call, also, and certainly they have enemies enough.

The answer could be in that these birds fly in groups and one way of keeping contact within the group is through the use of calls in times of rain, fog, and darkness.

In addition to communicating within the group the cries serve to alert other groups moving in the sky. Perhaps one of the answers to how birds migrate could be found in this use of cries whereby the older groups lead the younger ones.

All the birds that at times fly at night appear to use call notes. The shore birds and the duck family, the warblers, the sparrows, the thrushes—all are voluble on their night journeys.

Generally those birds who migrate by day are silent. Here the birds' remarkable ability to see great distances would assist them in following other birds.

In the opinion of some ornithologists, many birds have signals in their plumages whereby their presence is communicated to other birds by visual methods. An example of this would be the white rump of the Flicker, which can be seen at a great distance. However, since many birds do not have these plumage signals and get along well without them the theory is far from perfect. The call-note assumption seems to be on firmer ground.

As the migrating geese are known for the strangely appealing music of their calls they also are known for the V formation of their flight. Many writers have offered the theory that flying in this design assists the birds by setting up an air current in which it is easier to fly. The birds ahead are supposed to act as wind breakers, so to speak.

Certainly a number of larger birds fly in this formation but an equal number of larger birds, such as the Brant and the Snow Geese, do not use a tight formation. If it was the perfect flight pattern other birds would have evolved its use. Perhaps it is of some help but surely it is not overly effective.

VINCENT ABRAITYS

Loons, for instance, fly together but the distance between the birds is so great at times that no grouping whatsoever is discerned.

While on the subject of loons, it is worthy of note that I saw forty-six of these birds on Mountain Lake, which is up in Warren County, on an April 15th. The day was foggy and rainy and presumably the birds dropped to water because of the poor visibility.

All the birds were in bright Summer plumage. From the group came sporadic loon yelps, a strange eerie sound here on an inland lake so developed by man. It was not the full call of the Maine lakes but it was the first time I recall having heard the loon cry in New Jersey.

Many observers have noted the twisting and turning of flocks of small sandpipers in flight over the beaches. An obvious conclusion for this erratic flight pattern is that predators such as hawks find it difficult to follow a single bird in a twisting, turning group.

Another theory given is that the birds wish to maintain a group and their twisting in air allows the slow ones, the laggards, to keep up with the main body simply by cutting across the curves of flight which gives them a shorter distance to fly at all times.

It is obvious to anyone who keeps up on the literature of birds, or any wild life for that matter, that for any behavior seen some one somewhere has advanced a theory for this behavior. All the theories have some merit. Few will ever be proven. Yet the speculation is interesting.

That the grouping of birds in air has some defensive attributes may be deduced by the action of our common Starlings when one of the accipitrine, or bird hawks, pass over the sky. This action in which the birds rise to a tight group to fly around the hawk has been seen by many. The birds swirl around the hawk like a swarm of bees. They circle the hawk almost as if baiting it, now to one side, now above. The flock will even pass directly before the hawk.

To my mind the Starlings give a police escort to an enemy over the sky safely past their abodes. The hawk knows he is in no danger since he loafs along at his usual speed. Yet the hawk never makes an attempt to capture one of the Starlings. Perhaps from experience he knows that this is futile. The entire process is one of those oddities of nature that no one quite satisfactorily explains.

One of the obvious truths of life on this planet is that birds fly under their own power. This is something that man for all his intelligence has not been able to do. But man continually speculates on this ability in birds.

It may be that because of this inability man is unable absolutely to comprehend the behavior of birds in flight. It may be that every theory advanced on bird behavior so far is wrong in every aspect. It does not matter. Birds continue to fly with unconcern for man. Man continues to be charmed by the glide and power in bird wing, by the graceful sweep of pinion across the sky, by the sound of birds passing in season.

On Avoiding Snakes

I saw a black snake cross the road the other day, and I was reminded how slow snakes actually travel. A child could have walked across the road faster than this reptile, and the snake was in a hurry.

On seeing a snake most of us focus our eyes on the rapid sideward movement of the coils. The sideward motion is violent and gives the appearance of great speed. But the forward motion is very slow by comparison with this side twisting. This movement must be an excellent camouflage. Certainly the dangerous, or critical, section of a snake is the head, but the eye is drawn to the coils.

No local snake can travel faster than an active child or adult. On observing the speed of some people on sighting a snake, I would say the snake does not exist that can compete with a human's flight. Most of our non-poisonous snakes and most of our poisonous ones, too, gladly scatter at the approach of a human if given the opportunity. At rare times, however, they will remain still, hoping that their protective coloration or concealment will let the intruder pass by harmlessly.

But all the wild has a tolerance distance at which movement begins. Should one come within the tolerance distance of a non-poisonous snake, it will suddenly burst into flight. In the case of a poisonous snake, it will strike so fast the eye cannot follow the movement and then move slowly away, for our poisonous snakes cannot travel rapidly. All the measures they take are defensive.

Of course, in the out-of-doors anything can happen, but avoiding snakes can be a matter of training.

The first rule is to travel slowly but not silently. Snakes hear best through the solid contact of earth so the heavy footfall is picked up at a considerable distance. This allows the reptile plenty of time to move out of the path of the stroller.

This does not make unnecessary the use of the eyes, still our best organ of sense. Watch where you step is a good axiom for snakes and for everything else in the woods and fields. Avoid climbing where the hands are used for holds which the eye cannot see. Rocky slopes and ledges are apt to have a higher proportion of snakes than the leafy forest floor. Avoid brushing against stone walls or reaching into any crevice. In other words, use extreme caution in any stony or rocky area.

Since snakes like concealment during the day, dense shrubs or weedy thickets are also under suspicion. Look where you step, watch where you place your hands, move slowly and heavily and it will be almost impossible to come upon a snake, much less be in danger from it. If you go blundering around at night, all bets are off.

Our northern poisonous snakes rarely discharge enough venom to be fatal and since venom is replaced slowly they are not overly anxious to deplete their supply. As one goes further south the snakes are larger, the period of hibernation shorter, the venom more dangerous, and the reptiles more inclined to use their fangs.

Panic can be a great factor in the effects of snake bite. Generally, all carefully taught, complicated first-aid rules will be forgotten, so the essential one of calmness should be stressed. If bitten, move towards medical assistance without delay, calm in the assurance that your life expectancy is still greater than the snake's.

I believe it was the late, fine naturalist Alan Devoe who wrote that upon receiving a poisonous snake bite one ought to sit on a stump and smoke a cigarette completely before making a move. The point he was stressing was the quelling of the inevitable panic that will attempt to seize us all in this circumstance.

Never Trust a Botanist for Directions

Never trust a botanist for directions. Likely you will either starve to death in the woods or wind up in the middle of some town's Main Street.

People used to the woods have an offhand attitude toward the land. Landmarks tend to be a personal thing—a big rock, an old hemlock, a boggy swale, a clump of laurel. Points in a botanist's mind tend to be as lasting as the deed descriptions of a century ago where lines, for instance, ran from a chestnut stump to a pile of stones.

This was brought to me forcefully in an endeavor to locate a bog in Morris County. This bog has the distinction of harboring the only

Timber Rattlesnake

THE BACKYARD WILDERNESS

station in New Jersey of Ledum groenlandicum, the Labrador Tea.

Many people have been into this Ledum bog and I received as many sets of directions, all of them vague. They involved old railroad beds, streams running this way and that, various roads dirt and otherwise, and many compass directions.

I did meet one honest man who stated that I had better get someone to lead me to the spot since he remembered nothing.

The last person I talked to on the subject was Lee Edwards and he, at least, placed me on a correct road, a small dirt road north of Dover. He admitted his inadequacy thereafter but gave me a background of swamps on left and swamps on right and ridges running in various directions.

I found that in a general way he was correct. He did have the right road.

But all those conflicting directions were of small consequence since somehow or other in the woods one develops an instinctive feel for the land which leads the feet to spots of which no prior knowledge is had. I might put it this way. A botanist never knows where he is or was but is never lost. He is unable to direct one to a specific spot but unhesitatingly he himself will get there. The condition is baffling and difficult of explanation.

Since I wanted to see this stand I was on the road to which Edwards directed me at 7:30 of a rainy, foggy morning. I plunged into the woods alone and trusted to instinct. I circled about swampy areas and went up and down small ridges in the fog crossing a stream along the way.

In due time I saw an area which suited what I had in mind for a Labrador Tea bog. Off in the center was a fine stand of our American Larch just breaking into bud.

This Spring has been wet and the bog was sodden. Water stood everywhere in blackish pools. Since in April water is cold I had taken the precaution of wearing waders so I was not daunted.

I made a complete circle of the bog first looking for a path into it or perhaps an easy way through the wall-like shrubbery. I didn't find it. So I sighed and plunged into a foot of water that soon became two and slowly fought my way through the dense tangle of sapling, brush, and shrub.

Actually, in April before the leaves are out is the best time for a project like this since one can still see upwards and outwards somewhat and I had lined up a tall Sour Gum for a heading. I made the floating bog mat in the center on a straight line.

It is a small bog mat without open water and only slightly quaking so late in the stage it is. The diameter is only 20 or 30 feet. Here Leather Leaf was already in bloom with its small white bells and Pitcher Plants were greening nicely.

The Labrador Tea was a fine stand, an old stand to be sure, but a fine stand. It was in bud and sometime I would like to see the bloom, but the satisfaction of the thick, evergreen leaves with their felty undercoating was enough. Mission accomplished.

Nothing extraordinary was in bloom in these woods at this date and nothing else caught my eye except a solitary Black Spruce in an adjacent swamp. Perhaps the only other plant of interest was the Marsh Marigold which was here abundant. I returned to the car in the rain and fog without incident.

How does one get into this Ledum bog? Believe me, I haven't the faintest idea.

Basic Equipment for Birders

A number of people will have been fortunate enough to receive bird books as gifts. Those who already have Peterson's will be pleased to get any book on birds, for the true devotee will read anything on the subject.

Roger Tory Peterson's eastern *A Field Guide to the Birds* should be the first book and the essential one for the beginner. It is also the final authority for even the experienced birder. Peterson lists all the birds to be found in this area. The descriptions are concise and to the point. Furthermore, the plates are as near perfect as can be obtained, the colors good and the contours exact. Each illustration is marked with points for checking purposes. These are the field marks which not only identify the bird but serve to distinguish that bird from all others.

The Audubon Guides are good but are not as helpful in field work and the plates, while colorful, lack the precision of Peterson and thus the illustrations are not overly reliable. The Audubon Guides, though, have excellent summaries on each bird. The species notes are authoritative, informative, and make for marvelous reading on Winter evenings. The Guides are an excellent supplement to the handy Peterson.

Questions on binoculars are as frequent as those on bird books for only those who use them often have a good knowledge of their mechanics. It can be stated emphatically that the binoculars coming

THE BACKYARD WILDERNESS

out of Japan and sold under various manufacturers' names are completely reliable, and they are reasonably priced.

Since binoculars are to be used as a tool it would not pay to be too thrifty here but a good grade of small glasses can be gotten for well under a hundred dollars, but to go too low is a waste of money.

For those who intend to use binoculars at house windows or the comparatively short range of tree tops and nearby fences the 6 x 30 is adequate. The first number is the magnification and the second is the width of the light-admitting lens in millimeters. This second number determines the light factor, or in simple terms, how clearly an object will be seen.

Dividing the first number into the second, 6 into 30, gives 5, which is the light factoring number. One ought not to buy binoculars under a factor of 5. This means that as magnification increases the millimeter width should also increase. The binocular specifications best suited for field work are 6 x 30, 7 x 35, 7 x 50, and 8 x 40.

One should not work with high magnification in the beginning. It is much more difficult to handle and one ought to understand that if binoculars have not been used previously it may take a year or two to become proficient in their use. Get small glasses at first, practice, and be patient.

Once having a pair of 6 x 30s and a Peterson guide the next step is to lure the birds into a viewing area. Bird food is big business today and the advice of someone in the business is generally sound.

Bird food can best be standardized in three categories, suet, sunflower seed, and chick scratch. Suet is relished by all birds with the exception of confirmed seed eaters. Animal fat is the yardstick of survival for most species in the cold Winter. Suet brings in quantities of chickadees and titmice, Myrtle Warblers, woodpeckers, and nuthatches.

Sunflower seed, while also relished by many birds, is a specialty food for the thick-billed finches. It brings in the Purple Finches, Cardinals, goldfinches, siskins, and Evening Grosbeaks.

The finely cracked corn and wheat which is known everywhere as chick scratch is for the host of sparrows. The juncos, the Tree, Field, Chipping, Song, and White-throated Sparrows like small seeds and will winter well on them.

There are many other foods which can be added to the basic ones. These include ground meats, peanut butter mixed with cornmeal, fruits of all kinds, and every variety of seed known to commerce. The choice is up to the individual budget.

To hold birds, habit must be induced. Once food is put out, the supply should be maintained. To get the maximum number of species it should be placed at several spots and at varying heights. In time it will be found that birds will frequent certain feeders almost to the exclusion of others.

It is important that at least one feeding area be close to a thicket hedge or evergreen. Few birds like to feed completely in the open where they are exposed to attack from above. A shelter close by will relax even the most timid of birds.

Water is important. In some areas birds will be more dependent on the water supply than on the food. In Winter, fresh water should be put out frequently so an unfrozen supply is always about.

Conforming to the above directions should give a Winter full of birds seen from the comfort of homes. Even if all the birds are not identified correctly they will furnish hours of relaxation and entertainment.

Hawk Watching

A certain breed of birder is now beginning to come to the fore. It is the hawk watcher, the ridge strider.

Still in the humidity of mid-August this birder knows that the raptores are moving, that those birds who breed in Labrador and in the northern spruce forests have left that land of short Summer and are infiltrating the mountains of our eastern states.

So this birder now betakes himself sweatily to the high points of our eastern states. He climbs the hot, rocky trails with enthusiasm and arrives at the peaks breathless from the climb and his own anticipation.

This thing is occurring at Mount Tom and Bear Mountain and along the Shawangunk. It is at Montclair Quarry and Chimney Rock, at Sunrise Mountain and Raccoon Ridge. It is also at Mount Minsi and Lehigh Gap, at Bake Oven Knob and Hawk Mountain. We know it occurs farther down at Carlisle in Sterrett's Gap and a series of places that are only names.

Now this hawk watcher gets upon these high rocks and he sits there. He has his lunch with him and a pad and pencil. Throughout the day he scans the northeast sky.

At his spot it is pleasant. In the valley it is hot and close but here the air is light and cool. The distant sounds of the valley's life come as from a remote, other land.

Broad-winged Hawks

THE BACKYARD WILDERNESS

It is isolated here, where the full sky is open and the scene is of a countryside below. Sometimes I wonder if the hawks alone bring the birder here.

In August and September the Bald Eagles move strongly. Perhaps most of these are the eagles of our southern states such as Florida who are going down to nest along the coasts. But some of them are the eagles of Maine and eastern Canada who are going down to the Great Smokies and the other southern ranges, perhaps even to Mexico, to spend the Winter on sunnier beaches and hills.

Broad-winged Hawks are moving. The Broad-wings always move early for all of our Broad-wings leave us for the Winter. Some of them will spend the season as far down as the upper part of South America.

A kettle of Broad-wings swirling like dust-blown leaves upward to the zenith beyond the eyes' reach is fine compensation for a rocky climb.

Red-shoulders will drift by and Red-tails. Surprisingly, some of the falcons are moving, too. Scores of Sparrow Hawks will be seen and, rarely, the magnificent Duck Hawk, symbolic of all that is powerful and swift in the bird world, will delight our eyes in its passing.

The Marsh Hawks will ease by lazily. They are never in a hurry and invariably fly close to tree-top level.

All birds are moving. Past the lookout points will go hummingbirds and crows, Blue Jays and darting warblers. All the birds that migrate by day like to follow the high ridges and many of the nighttime migrants will move during the day.

It is wonderful to spend a hot Summer day on the cool rocks above the shimmering haze in the lowlands but in the Autumn it is finer still. In the Fall the movement of birds over the blazes of October's wood appears more natural. The sense is of coming Winter.

The Broad-wings will have gone by then and many of the Sharp-shins. All the other hawks will be represented though, and to these will be added those splendid visitants, the Goshawk and the Golden Eagle.

In this season the ridge-sitter will have all of October's splendor below him and in the sky will be the splendid birds. It is no wonder that the hawk watcher will make the arduous hike and consider it worthwhile and will return again and again.

Perhaps the birder on the high boulders in hot August thinks ahead to the cold gusts of November driving the brown leaves on these rocks, but most likely he thinks with satisfaction of three months of pleasure ahead on the ridges.

VINCENT ABRAITYS

Big Day

In birding there is a fantastic thing called Big Day. Big Day is a comparatively new project in the bird world being perhaps 30 years old.

It is not too well favored. Only a handful of birders ever get in on one, mostly because of its demands on time and energy and the need for a sharp knowledge of birds and the geography of birds to make it worth the while.

There is nothing official about a Big Day. Anyone can make a Big Day at any time and anywhere. The whole affair is purely artificial.

After a Big Day is complete it has proved nothing except that as one gets older it takes a little longer to recover from the lack of sleep and the extreme physical exertion.

Briefly, this is the procedure on a Big Day. Within any 24-hour period in May an attempt is made to find the greatest number of different kinds of birds. One may go anywhere on this project but one must respect the 24-hour limit. Early May is chosen because the greatest number of birds are found in any one spot at this time of year.

Howard Drinkwater, Henry Barlow, and myself made our Big Day on May 12th. Since no one of the three had any intention of staying awake for 24 hours, each of us began about 5:30 in the morning.

Barlow began at Oldwick and proceeded to Whitehouse where he picked up Drinkwater and on the way to Flemington to pick me up they made several side trips. I began at Sergeantsville and worked northward to Point Breeze and thence down to Flemington where we now came together at 6:30 in the morning.

We went southward via Reaville and the top of the Sourland and it was 7 A.M. when we left Hunterdon County. The morning was not ideal. Birds could be heard but a wandering fog cut down visibility. Warblers were absent. Nonetheless, when we left Hunterdon County we already had 55 species of birds on our list.

This is impressive but it means little at this time of day. This is always the best time of day to census birds and this rate is never maintained later in the day. Furthermore, weather conditions would have to get better. Wind and the direction of wind always makes or breaks a Big Day. At seven in the morning the weather looked none too perfect.

By nine o'clock we were at the entrance to Brigantine National

THE BACKYARD WILDERNESS

Wildlife Refuge, some 90 miles away from Flemington. We now had 70 species of birds on the list. At this rate our goal of 150 species would be reached easily. Or so we thought.

We met Jim Meritt of Blackwood here. Jim was scouting the area for Camden and Philadelphia area birders' Big Day. Jim was done when we met him for he was going home to sleep. Their Big Day was to go for 24 hours and they were to start at 10:30 that evening. They would move down to the upper part of the State of Delaware to begin with owls. Thence they would move across southern Jersey.

I did not check whether they would hit the Poconos also but the Philadelphia birders generally wind up in the mountains. Crossing three states is a rugged schedule and I do not envy them.

Their goal was 200, 50 more than ours. This is a high figure and it was doubtful that it would be reached since Jim reported poor prospects at the refuge.

We covered the dikes and woods adjacent to the salt marshes and we birded until one o'clock and when we stopped for lunch our count was 120. A good figure, but we now knew we would never hit our goal of 150 since we had exhausted the possibilities here.

The wind had changed. It swung over to the north and east and it was cold. An overcast hid the sun. Birds had stopped flying and had stopped calling. We were licked. After eating and until two o'clock when we left for Tuckerton we added only five birds. Warblers were absent here and the shore birds just were not around.

Some of the other bird families cooperated beautifully though. Our raptore count was good with the immature Bald Eagle and Peregrine on it. The heron count was good. We got the Glossy Ibis, Cattle Egret, Yellow-crowned Night Heron, and American Bittern, all scarce members. The duck-goose family gave us a dozen species.

But we were missing out on the common birds like the cormorant and late migrants. We got no Pectoral Sandpipers nor any semi-rare species. We left the refuge with 125 species.

Tuckerton was a bust. A full hour was wasted on this trip out to the Coast Guard station on Great Egg Harbor Bay. Not a single new bird was added. We started home and near the Garden State Parkway we added a pair of Red-tailed Hawks.

We spent some time at Walnford in the marl belt below Allentown, New Jersey. This spot gave us only the White-breasted Nuthatch. It should have given us about ten species. A stop near Princeton added the Warbling Vireo. It was not even singing. The fields in the Amwell Valley south of Flemington should have given us a half-dozen more. They produced absolutely nothing.

We wound up with 129 species. This is a respectable figure for 13 hours of birding but it fell short of the 139 of the year previous. It was not even close to our hope of 150.

I would say that the weather was poor but there was nothing to be done about that. The bird families that let us down were the warblers, finches, and blackbirds. Possibly a lot of these birds were around but were not singing. Possibly they had not yet arrived.

Oh well, we'll try it again next year. I think we ought to set our goal for 175 and do a little scouting beforehand. Maybe we ought to try for two cars of birders if we can find volunteers for this mild form of madness.

Rock Hounding

I can recommend rock hounding for the cold days of Winter. Pounding stone is warming and the exercise is beneficial. However, it is not much of a hobby for someone with bursitis. It can be a little tiring, too.

It is hard on clothes. There is a tendency to stuff delectable but hard-edged specimens into pockets, and a group of rock hounds leaving a quarry has a positive waddle. But once at home, discarded specimens can be used to build a fireplace or a stone wall or to patch the lane, so it has its rewards.

Temperley, Ferguson, Robinson, and I moved a good portion of the Swayze dumps recently just looking. Temperley assured us there were some wonderful rocks here where pyrite, olivine, and magnetite were colorfully associated in a silver, black, and green combination. We found pyrites and olivine and lots of magnetite but not in combination, so I suppose this was the usual pie in the sky thing he got at sixth hand.

Rock hounds have a special manner of speech and a unique routine. It goes like this. A piece of rock is tossed to the person on the right with an exclamation, "Hey, look at this." That person comments in this fashion, "Beautiful, really beautiful," before tossing it on. Responses follow down the line, "I didn't know it occurred here" or "The State Geologist ought to see this" or "Amazing," until it returns to the finder who then callously throws it away.

THE BACKYARD WILDERNESS

I have never been able to determine what these extraordinary rocks were. Whenever I have asked pertinent questions the hammering has increased and no one has heard me over the din.

Arnitz, Temperley, MacNamara, Drinkwater, and I helped reduce the elevation of Jugtown Mountain on a Sunday. We started at the quarry along the highway. It is amazing the number of minerals that can be found among the fresh rock of this area. The gneiss is interlaced with pegmatite dikes, faults, and seams which are highly productive to the mineralogist.

Pyrite and marcasite, chlorite mica and muscovite, olivine, asbestos fibers, serpentine, manganese stains, quartz crystals, graphic granite—all occur.

We went on to inspect the enormous cut and fill of the new highway over Jugtown. No one expected that the Kittatinny limestone which was encountered in the railroad tunnel would be exposed at the comparatively minor depth of the cut, but no one knows what can be found in fresh stone, so the search is always exciting.

The future traveler will see near the center of the cut a fine exposure of a narrow dike slicing up through the gneiss, black and contrasting in textbook perfection.

The entire eastern end of the new gap is through a huge pegmatitic dike. This is largely microcline. It looks like calcite, but it is a potassium aluminum silicate as opposed to a calcium carbonate. Microcline breaks down to kaolinite, a commercial clay.

The microcline is shot through with hornblende, the black of hornblende contrasting sharply with the light-colored microcline. Some of the hornblende crystals run four to six inches in length, but unfortunately cannot be removed as such from the matrix.

While this new cut through the mountain is impressive, the fill is spectacular for this section of the country. On completion this will be a scenic bit of highway.

As we were returning to our cars we encountered another party with the usual pockets full of rocks and bags full of rocks, and hospitality demanded that we inspect each others' finds. This group had been checking the fresh cuts on weekends all through the Winter. They were picking up the same things that we were, but in addition had amassed some striking pyrite samples.

Our last stop was the quarry at Pattenburg. Three radioactive minerals have been found here—Allanite, Fergusonite, and Polycrase. The Geiger counter was unpacked.

Since the sun was dropping low in the west, I left the party here and have not since ascertained whether the die-hards were successful.

VINCENT ABRAITYS

Birds Unseen but Heard

So many of our more interesting birds are rarely seen. They are a voice, a disembodied sound from the treetops or the thickets and are never identified. If people could but learn the sounds of birds so many more would be known and enjoyed.

I know of no cure for the situation but practice and work and help perhaps from someone who already knows the songs and call notes. The records of bird songs are fine for some people but most people, including myself, cannot relate the record sounds to the living songs.

I am reminded of this through the song of a bird here at home whom I never see. He is a constant singer and has been for some weeks but I have not caught a glimpse of him. In this case it is not necessary because I know the bird is a Yellow-throat.

Many birders call this little warbler the Maryland Yellow-throat but this is out of fashion since the experts say it is incorrect. They say the Maryland is a mere subspecies and cannot be distinguished in the field from the Northern Yellow-throat, especially in migration. Therefore, the birds are to be properly called Yellow-throat Warblers.

The Yellow-throat is a ground warbler, an abundant one. It breeds in thickets, fence lines, and on stream sides. It likes damp situations but is not particular about this as a requirement.

The Yellow-throat male is a handsome fellow. He is basically yellow in color but has a black mask across the eyes like the proverbial burglar. He is small, about as big as a Chipping Sparrow.

The song of the Yellow-throat is a "witchity-witchity-witchity" phrasing given many times and once the song is known the presence of the bird is known. Like the Indigo Bunting, it is surprising how many of them are really about.

The bird I have here tends to follow me about on my saunters. Whether this is curiosity, territorial antagonism, or friendliness I am not sure. Perhaps it is a mixture of all three.

At any rate, I can hear his song from the apple tree, the raspberry thickets, or the goldenrods always close by and I know he is near. Normally he has some singing perches close to the road and I suspect that the nest is there in the weeds.

THE BACKYARD WILDERNESS

This is one of the birds which we have here annually and really never bother with. We always hear the "witchity-witchity-witchity" and it is so common we generally pass it by. Long may the species stay this common.

III

Wet Places

A Lesson to be Learned from a Pennsylvania Bog

At nights now the coons are on the road. The Autumn rains start all animals prowling. A restlessness pervades wild life at this season, the restlessness of cold.

A traveler through the less settled regions of New Jersey quickly finds that much land has been acquired by the Scouts, YMCA groups, and various others.

These camps and the acreage surrounding them have not been developed in our accepted sense of tampering with the natural state of things. No attempt has been made in a senseless desire to improve on Nature. True conservation has been followed, which is a completely hands-off attitude.

While much praise should accrue to these groups for their pure approach to the practice of conservation, a much more important point should be emphasized. The Scout, YMCA, and church groups that have set up these wild areas have been led and are being led by people of deep and discerning insight into the future.

They have acted for their own groups quickly and forthrightly. They saw that open land was disappearing from the state. They recognized the need of such land for their youth and they acquired it.

If such a thing is good for high-minded groups why then is it not also a good thing for the populace at large? If boards of directors are able to set aside open space for select groups why should not county governments set aside open space for all the people within their jurisdictions?

It is impossible to set a price on the color of a tree in October, the sound of a stream running down a hillside, the flash of bird wing in May, but there are manners in which repayment is made.

Let us go back to the year of our Great Flood, 1955, I believe it was, and recall the tragedy in the Brodhead and Marshalls Creek areas in the foothills of the Poconos.

The devastation was beyond calculation and the count in human lives enormous. Even today the evidences remain and even today bodies have not yet been found.

Across a ridge from Brodhead Creek is the small town of Tannersville. A considerable stream comes to Tannersville from a northeasterly direction and this stream penetrates the Tannersville Bog. The bog is a large area of quaking earth and it is famous in a botanical way, but outside of an occasional botanist and a few Pocono bears no one uses it. It appears to be a large area going to waste.

And so some people thought and they began a movement to drain and develop the Tannersville Bog. But in a way unusual for country folk, the residents of the Tannersville area suddenly decided that they did not want to lose their bog. Maybe it was not making money for anyone but they liked it anyway and they fought this thing out and they saved their bog.

Came the rain and the flood. While bodies, barns, bridges, and boulders rolled down Brodhead Creek and in all the other creek valleys in appalling enormity, Tannersville became unique. No lives were lost in the Tannersville Bog valley, no bridges went out, no barns went downstream. Their hitherto useless bog became an enormous sponge that held water in fabulous quantities and released it slowly and damage was virtually unknown.

What of Tannersville Bog today? Well, only an occasional botanist and a few Pocono bears still slog their way into this watery wilderness and it is still not making money for anyone. But it has paid its way many times over.

So with all open space, all land that to the careless eye or the material eye seems to be serving only the coon, the salamander, and the Blue Jay, who knows when land of this character will be the salvation of the spirit of the young of tomorrow or, perhaps, even their lives.

On nights of northeast rain when yellow leaves slick the country roads the coons cross the highways and the possums may be seen on the roadside banks and the deer go hunting for frosted apples on the hills.

An Abundance of Birds

Bird enthusiasts who wish to enlarge on their knowledge are fortunate in having an extensive New Jersey coast line to explore.

The water boundary of the state begins at the north with the Hudson River estuary and moves southward via the tidal runs and inlets of the metropolitan area. Southward from the expanse of Raritan Bay is the

THE BACKYARD WILDERNESS

ocean proper with wide marshlands fringing the sand beaches and dunes. Close to a hundred miles of ocean front is available to birders in this state.

From Cape May northward and inland is the area of Delaware Bay and the tidal river to Trenton. On the fresh water large numbers of shore and water birds may be seen well upward into Hunterdon County.

We are fortunate in having almost every type of water habitat suitable for birds. These ideal factors are reflected in the long list of birds which have been recorded in the state.

At times we rural folk are a bit patronizing toward the residents of our built-up northeastern counties, assuming that because they are in congested cities they have no opportunity to study birds.

We need not feel too sorry for our city brethren when it comes to opportunities for seeing birds. By and large, in certain classes of birds they are better off than we are.

Nowhere else on the eastern coast of the United States may one find such an abundance of sheltered waters as in northeastern New Jersey. One has the opportunity here of New York Bay and the lower Hudson, of Newark Bay and the lower reaches of the Hackensack and Passaic Rivers, of Kill Van Kull and the Arthur Kill.

The availability of all these waters ranging from fresh through brackish to salt is seen in the fine list of birds entered by these urban birders who never leave the bounds of their cities. Especially in Winter do they outstrip country bird watchers in their gull lists and duck lists. These areas are better for seeing gulls and ducks than any other place on the eastern coast.

Actually, it is considered that the lower Raritan and Raritan Bay is the beginning boundary for coastal New Jersey and most birders begin at this spot.

The waters between New Brunswick and Sandy Hook provide the largest Winter concentration of the Canvasback Duck in the state. It also shelters the largest rafts of scaup, and it usually teems with the northerly Golden-eye Duck in the Winter months.

Gulls of all species, the common and the rare, may be seen on Raritan Bay now and Horned Grebes and many of the commoner ducks.

From Sandy Hook on down the number of good birding spots is legion. The estuaries of the Navesink and Shrewsbury Rivers are excellent as is Lake Takanassee in Long Branch. Asbury Park gives us Deal Lake and then we have small but productive Sylvania Lake in Bradley Beach.

Ornithological literature carries many times the names of Wreck

Pond and Lake Como and Old Sam's Pond in Point Pleasant. Manasquan Inlet is a good spot to look for birds as is Shark River Inlet.

But along the coast more different birds have been reported from the Shark River estuary than from any other spot on the north shore. Shark River is still tops and any birder who passes it by while shore birding in Winter is not doing justice to his hobby. Furthermore, almost all the shoreline of Shark River is accessible by road and the birder need never leave his car.

The good birder along this section of coast never neglects the ocean. The ocean ought to be scanned periodically for Gannets or Kittiwakes and the area just beyond the surf bears particular scrutiny for loons and grebes and alcids. The stone jetties that project into the surf are fine places for Purple Sandpipers and along their edges are where the Harlequin Ducks feed and the Common and King Eider, should any be in the area.

The beaches and the towns that have the most people in Summer are the best birding spots in the Winter. The birds take over in the Winter and the bird watcher thinks the arrangement is just fine for in Winter he is not disturbed by people or traffic.

Slogging in a Pond

Through fortuitous circumstances I have had occasion to spend much more than usual time this Summer in the southern Jersey counties of Ocean, Burlington, Atlantic, and Cape May. So far I have been stung and bitten by mosquitoes, green flies, deer flies, ticks, chiggers, yellow jackets, and a small, black underwater beetle with fire in its tail.

The interlude from the leafy waves of hills in Hunterdon with their rocky texture to flat sand, slow river, bog, marsh, pond, swamp, and dune with their wholly dissimilar flora, foreign to Hunterdon, carrying a southern tone, has been completely fascinating.

I recall an evening in company with a botanist from Pleasantville when we worked a new area west of Scullville. It was the familiar routine of driving down a macadam road to a sand road and then driving down the sand road till it was no more. Then we waded a cattail swamp and moved into a wood heavy with Sweet Gum and Sour Gum, Persimmon, holly, and Spanish Oak. We came to a small dune in the forest forming a knoll and in among the heather and lichens

THE BACKYARD WILDERNESS

I found several jasper chips and a half dozen shards of Indian pottery, the like of which I have not seen in Hunterdon.

Beyond the dune was our objective, a vegetation-choked, swamp-like pond, and this we entered, and into hip-deep water among the tussock growth. Surrounding us were the great, flat flowers of Rose Mallow, big as tea cups, and in the air was the camphor smell of bruised Fleabane as we moved along.

A Snowy Egret left the area as we entered and the Fish Crows took to milling above us. As night deepened Night Herons squawked in transit through the air. There was no other sound but the slogging of our legs through water and the splash of countless frogs ahead of us.

Actually, this swamp pond was a bust. We found few things of interest beyond the usual, except for a remarkable growth of Poison Ivy upon the tussocks. The water was neither fresh nor salt, being in a marginal area.

Having lost our way in the gloom, we fought back through immense thickets of holly, greenbrier, and bramble. Now I cannot say whether it is worse to be ripped by countless thorns or drilled by those special marsh mosquitoes. We stopped at a clean, fresh pond on the way home and waded around to wash the stench from our clothes. A satisfying evening's work.

On another day we visited a pond between Egg Harbor City and Mays Landing. In the party was David Fables, Frank and Robert Hirst, and Bayard Long. The same routine prevailed. Down a sand road, park the car, and walk.

Our route took us through an old burn now water-logged in this year's wet Summer. A heavy growth of mosses formed tree to tree carpeting, the first step in the rejuvenation forest. Already the shrubs had moved back in—Leather Leaf, blueberry, huckleberry, wintergreen. Here and there the pines were resprouting.

A pond such as this one is a depression with no inlet or outlet, depending on surface water, and varying in depth with the rainfall. We have nothing like it where I live. The bottom is hard sand with only a minor accumulation of decaying plant life. Walking through such quiet water with its sand bottom is easy.

The bottom surface of such a pond supports many algae and plants such as Mermaid-weed and bladderwort. Breaking the surface of the water is an abundant grass, the Maiden Cane. This is the absolute northern point for the growth of this grass.

The pond was on our schedule for the two good plants it possesses—Boykin's Lobelia and the Awned Meadow Beauty, Rhexia aristosa. Both plants root in the sandy bottom and send stems up to the surface.

Once through the surface they bloom, the Lobelia with typical small, blue flowers, but the Rhexia with four huge, showy, pink petals.

On this day careful study was made of an odd, small bladderwort. It was quite minute, and the well-formed flower was hardly a sixteenth of an inch long. No one in the group recognized it, the consensus being that it was a hitherto undescribed variant or an entirely new species.

Perhaps in the foregoing paragraphs I have answered partially the old question: Why does a person climb a mountain? Or, in this case, why does a fully clothed, reasonably sensible adult go slogging around in a pond?

Finding a Mole Cricket

There are times when out of small disappointments there may come still appeasing satisfactions. I had such an experience lately when I tried to collect a plant I had noted some months before in a tiny pool atop of Kittatinny.

The plant was a Water Starwort, a pretty name for a most nondescript plant. Generally it is a rosette of leaves which floats inconspicuously in quieter waters. In the axils of the leaves, that is where the leaf meets the stem, a small flower produces a small seed, the green of the flower matching exactly the green seed.

Since at the time I first noted the Water Starwort it was sterile as to seed and flower and these are needed for a smart identification of the species, I returned to gather these only to find that the pool had dried completely because we had no rainfall and the aquatic phase of the plant had gone of necessity to the terrestrial stage.

Disappointedly, I gathered some gobs of the mud in which the plants grew and took them home and, as I suspected, there were no seeds when I searched for them under a hand lens. On the paper over which I had strewn my specimens I became aware of a small creature which was crawling about most dejectedly. The tiny muddied and bewildered creature which now had all of my attention proved to be a Mole Cricket, an insect I had never seen before but which I understand is a good find if you are a cricket fancier.

The cricket crawled slowly on this strange surface in insect befuddlement which I could understand from the rough handling it had received in the previous 24-hour period.

Mole Cricket

THE BACKYARD WILDERNESS

While the abduction of the Mole Cricket was purely accidental, nonetheless I felt a certain responsibility to the innocent victim so I gathered it up carefully and took it out to the roadside ditch which looked protectively damp and there I deposited it. Hopefully, it will find friends.

Dowitchers and Peeps

At this time of year, late July, the narrow band of sand rimming the Atlantic Ocean is thronged with people from dawn to dusk and the birds of water have lost the surf until cooler weather.

But back of the dunes between the barrier beaches and the mainland is a wide expanse of marsh, salty and swarming with life, and a web of tidal channels replenishing the black, odorous mud flats in lunar regularity from the inexhaustible life of the sea.

The throb of migration has once again begun. The waves of piper and plover in inexorable beat flood upon the marsh, the sand flats and the mud flats. Beyond the swarms of people crowding the beach sands the legion of wings performs its ancient rite of the dwindling sun.

One of the earliest of the shore birds to arrive, one of the most abundant and most interesting, is the dowitcher. A few individuals are back by the last week of June and thereafter they pour in flock after flock throughout the Summer and into late Autumn.

The dowitcher is a chunky, little bird with the longest bill in proportion to its size of all the shore birds. Its bill is longer even than that of the Woodcock and Wilson's Snipe. In Spring it is rich red in color principally across the breast, but in Autumn it is a faded gray blending into the sands.

They are gentle birds and trusting, the flocks on the marshes feeding quietly about the observer. As is the habit of all sandpipers, individual birds and groups are always seeking better feeding spots so the air over the marshes and flats is filled continually with the fluttering of wings and the musical whinny of their voices.

The dowitcher is one of the few birds that retains a name of Indian origin, in this instance Iroquoian. It has always been one of the more important of the migrants to the Indian and the white man as a food source. Along with a series of its relatives, it was gunned extensively by the market huntsmen of a generation ago, but our present protective laws have brought it back in some number.

Its breeding groups are far north from western Alaska to Hudson Bay and from upper Manitoba and Alberta to the shores of the Arctic Ocean. Here it lines a little depression in a hummock with some grass and moss for its four eggs. The young forage on the treeless wet tundra and the oozing muskeg.

With us, they probe the mud and water with their long bills for a variety of foods. The long bills are plunged rapidly and vertically downward deeply in a stitching effect. Marine worms of all sorts are taken and water insects of all kinds in the larval stage, midges and crane, soldier, horse, brine, and dance flies. Snails and mollusks of small size and any and all crustacea are included. Seeds of the vegetation of the mud and salt flats vary the diet.

Occasionally a few attempt to winter on the Jersey coast but the usual wintering grounds are from the Carolinas and southward along the Gulf Coast and through the Caribbean into South America far down into Brazil and Peru. The usual companions of our dowitchers along the coastal strip are a species group of sandpipers, half the size of dowitchers, that are called collectively peeps.

The peep group, in decreasing order of frequency, consists of Semipalmated, Least, Western, and White-rumped Sandpipers, plus the Dunlin and Sanderling. Dows are big and hulking to the eye but the little peeps are a bewildering swarm of movement.

They are tiny, sparrow-like in size. Their plumage is a blending of gray, brown, and white. Once they cease their mouse-like running to freeze on the mud and sand they become lost to the eye. Their size is no deterrent to flight, however, for like the dows they breed near the Arctic Ocean on one continent and winter below the Equator on another.

The impact of all these small shore birds on man is neutral. Only the Eskimo and the Cree of the far north knows them well. On their breeding grounds their companions are only the lonely caribou, Gyrfalcons, and the Arctic Foxes. On their visits to our shores they frequent only a narrow band of unused, watery land a few miles in width at most.

But they bring a great charm to our living. They are an integral part of the vast life of the seas and the soggy sea edges. To man within his rigid, little circle the little pipers of Baffin Island and Keewatin traveling happily down to Patagonia are the intimations of the vastness of earth and the ceaselessness of time.

In the Field with the Hirst Brothers

It has been some time since I was afield botanizing with Frank and Robert Hirst. By way of identity, these two young men have become, within the space of a decade, the recognized authorities on the Pine Barren flora of New Jersey.

Their field work has reinstated many plants to the New Jersey list. They have discovered stations for plants not hitherto known to grow in the state. In addition, they have found at least one species completely new to the science of botany. Needless to say, I anticipated a day with them.

I drove down to Atlantic County early Sunday morning. At about 8:30 we were already moving westward across southern Jersey towards Salem County. Our project for the day was to rediscover Quercus lyrata, the Swamp Post Oak, a southerly species.

About 60 years ago a single tree was found near Riddleton, a small settlement which does not now appear on any map. Unfortunately, knowledge of the exact location was lost and no one since has seen the tree.

Near Elmer a side trip was made by us to a small lake to see the European Floating Heart. The Floating Hearts are plants which resemble Water Lilies but properly belong to the gentian grouping. The European Floating Heart has yellow flowers as opposed to the white of our native species. It probably has escaped from backyard lily pools or water gardens and is now known at a few spots from New York to Virginia. This lake, so far as we know, is the only station in New Jersey.

In this lake it made a profuse growth and the large, yellow blossoms sprinkled the pond surface.

Next we passed through an area near Alloway where the Hirst brothers showed me some woods which held excellent stands of the Chinquapin, the Dwarf Chestnut. The Chinquapin suffered severely in the great blight of a half century ago which wiped out our native chestnuts. For a time it was feared that the Dwarf Chestnut would also become extinct since for many years no one could locate stands of it.

Yet in these woods the shrub was abundant. Here it grows to a height of three or four feet with now and then a specimen that rises to ten feet. Many of the plants here showed some blight damage but this did not prevent a nut crop which on this September 2nd was nearing maturity.

Having looked at two good plants we went to Riddleton and searched for a brick factory that is no longer standing where we hoped to take a railroad siding which is no longer in existence.

We were successful in this phase. On either side of the old embankment in the woods were fine stands of many oaks. Pin, Black, Red, White, Spanish, Post, and Willow Oak grew profusely and many trees showed evidence of hybridization. We found no tree resembling the Swamp Post Oak. We discussed the possibility that some peculiar hybridization or crossing had produced a single specimen which was misidentified. Perhaps we were not in the correct wood. The subject of Quercus lyrata is still open.

We left the Riddleton woods to explore the Penton area east of Salem. Salem County is rich farming country and a drive down its roads among its long, flat fields is easy to enjoy. A pond near Penton was overgrown with American Lotus, Nelumbo lutea. This pond and an area near the mouth of Mannington Creek appears to carry all the American Lotus that grows in the southern part of the state. In leaf and in blossom it is tremendous in size, but like the Floating Heart family it is always quite local in distribution. Most observers think that this is an imported plant. Actually, it is a native plant despite its tropical, exotic appearance.

Since Salem was still in the grip of a drought a pond that we visited was almost dry. On the pond rim were several specimens of the Basket Oak and these were growing with the Swamp White Oak. The Basket, or Cow Oak, is a southern oak that I had seen previously only in the Double Pound Swamp of Cape May County. It appears at a few scattered sites through our southernmost counties.

Considering that in our drive through some of the sandier areas we passed the Scarlet Oak, Dwarf Chestnut Oak, Bearcat Oak, and Blackjack Oak, our oak list for the day showed a remarkable species range in this family.

In the long plant list for the day one other species stands out. This is Coreopsis rosea. It is a native Coreopsis, or Tickseed, that is a rare inhabitant of southern Jersey bogs. While I had seen the plant before, it had not been in bloom. This day I was shown a small bog heavy with rose-pink blossoms.

I was satisfied with the sight. The burden of the long drive back to Hunterdon County was lighter with the memory of southern Jersey blossomings, its Chinquapin woods, and the long, flat fields of Salem County.

THE BACKYARD WILDERNESS

The Shouting, Searching, Milling Throng

September opened in usual perfection. In the morning about the house there were two male Redstarts and a female, a pair of Cape May Warblers, a single male Wilson's Warbler, a young Yellow-throat, two Hummingbirds, a Cedar Waxwing, and a Wood Pewee.

Here off on a dirt road it was quiet and the green of this year's lush vegetation was heaped upon the countryside. After many days spent along the southern coastal strip of New Jersey during the Summer the contrast was a relief.

As usual, the seashore teemed this Summer. It teemed with people, heat, humidity, greenheads, and mosquitos. Each year sees the roads of the coast a little heavier with traffic than a year before. Each year the area clogs a little more.

And the building! From Oceanville to Absecon solid down to Somers Point is a vast building boom even stretching far inland along the many highways. Only the camouflaging pines hides to the casual eye this explosion on the sands.

Down near the airport above the race track a monstrous machine with spiked rollers as big as a house takes a huge swath through the pine forest as easily as a homeowner mows his lawn. The trees splinter like toothpicks.

Scattered about are numerous trailer parks with house trailers jammed side by side on the open sand, open to harsh sun. The trailer parks and the monotonous house-beside-house stretch even down to Cape May Point.

The people swarm. After the bumper to bumper incursion they spread out everywhere. The thousands make great clusters on the beaches, the sounds of them are a great roar over the surf, and the flocks of Laughing Gulls remain quiet and somber on Sundays.

All the waters are in regatta. The boats are as numerous as the Fiddler Crabs on the tidal mud. There are many species of boats, Greater Boats and Lesser Boats and a colorful host occupying all the available ecological niches of boatdom in between. They stream up Barnegat Bay and Great Bay, up the Mullica River to the consternation of the cormorants. They tow skiers in endless file up Great Egg Harbor River and the terns scream and scatter before them.

The people boat, they ski, they swim, they crab off the bridges, the crabbers clustering on the bridges to watch the crabs clustering on the bait in the water. The crabbers line the water transits, the guts and leads and channels, nets in hand, oblivious to the sun. Heron-like, in hunched patience, the fishermen watch their lines near to many herons and egrets but the varied appetite of the heron is the more easily satisfied and the fishermen continue to wait. The clammers on the sound always have the more action.

And on the sands of the beaches, on the salt marsh about the tidal waters, in among the pines and the holly the binoculared birder becomes no less a part of this eager, shouting, searching, progging, milling throng.

Now it is September and the seashore rests. And although September is perhaps the best of the year, it is also the saddest. The Harvest Fly that chirps on endlessly in the thicket advertises his own eulogy. The wasp that wades in gold upon the cosmos flies thence in doom.

For yet a while in bits of time the dwindling Summer sends a torrid messenger but Autumn seeps everywhere. Autumn is in the latening sunrise, the dews stay late in the morning, the bees are ten o'clock scholars. All vivid now are the gentians contending a chilling sun, their lurid purples ectoplasmic.

The falcons with whetted wings follow by day the warbler hordes that go by night beneath the aurora borealis, the ice-burning with its ancient tale of ice and glacier. The faintest of flames touches the hills groomed for October, a trace of yellow and purple runs along the fence lines.

The squirrels in the wood lot begin their quarrels over the hickory nuts. While the crabs and the clams along the shore are left alone and the boardwalks are finally cleaned of the Summer debris, inland there is the adjustment and anticipation of Autumn. Along the old fields on the hillsides the cock pheasant pecks at fallen apples on the browning grasses.

The Noblest of Wild Flowers

The Arethusa orchid to me is the noblest of wild flowers. There is a grandeur and dignity to its beauty.

The Summit Nature Club had a trip to the Pine Barrens, and in a bog below Whiting we found the Arethusa in perfect bloom. Memorial Day is the traditional time for its flowering in New Jersey although further north it may be delayed by the lateness of Spring.

Arethusa bulbosa

THE BACKYARD WILDERNESS

Here in the bog along Webb's Mill Brook it was especially abundant, as it has been for many years. There is some condition at this spot which is favorable to it, for while it is abundant here it is absent in most other southern Jersey bogs.

The common names for the Arethusa bulbosa are also Swamp Pink and Dragon's Mouth. However, since there is only one other species in the genus, and that one in Japan, the generic name of Arethusa seems preferable to American naturalists.

Orchids are hard to describe so I will not attempt it except to say that the Arethusa has a single blossom on a stem which is up to a foot high with sepals and petals of magenta-pink. The lip usually has white to yellow areas with crimson spots. The flower is large for a northern orchid.

We searched for the Curly Grass Fern at this spot. We were successful in finding some of last year's sterile and fertile fronds for study and the little watchspring beginnings of this year's sterile fronds, minute and eye-straining to locate.

Unless one sees how tiny is the Curly Grass Fern it is hard to imagine. It is really abundant here but one needs to have one's nose within a foot of the watery moss to find it.

Since water is such a cold medium there was little else in bloom in the bog. We found the three species of sundews which are here and we saw many Pitcher Plants coming into bloom.

The Summit Club had 18 cars in its group and about 50 people in the bog at one time. In addition, a camera club from Pennsylvania with nearly the same amount of people was working in the bog.

The camera enthusiasts were concentrating on the Arethusa with a few others working on the Pitcher Plants. Modern times has produced some sissy photographers. They now lay down sheets of plastic on which they kneel or squat to do their picture taking.

Later on in the day we encountered a large group of naturalists from Delaware. The bog was well trampled on this day.

There was more bloom on the sands than in the bog. The Hudsonia, or Beach Heather, was especially showy. Its golden blooms were in large patches along the road. Hudsonia also occurs along the shore on the sand dunes but there is now more of it inland on the sands than on the dunes. The Sand Myrtle was still in bloom and we were lucky enough to see some late Pyxie Moss. The huckleberries and the blueberries were blossoming and the Fetter Bush was in flower.

Turkey-beard was beginning to be colorful. This member of the Lily family is most grass-like in appearance when not in bloom. In June a central stem arises from the bottom cluster of grass-like leaves which then becomes covered with a large globular cluster of white flowers. Turkey-beard is another specialty of the Pines of New Jersey although it has a relative in the mountainous west in Bear Grass. Certainly the Pine Barrens at this time of year are far from barren in color.

In the afternoon we visited the West Plains, a vast area of stunted growth. Here we saw large patches of Bearberry and the specialty of the Plains, the Broom Crowberry. Here too the Beach Heather put on a magnificent display.

We did see southern Jersey's two birds of note, the Pine Warbler and the Prairie Warbler, which with the Arethusa, the Curly Grass Fern, and the flowering shrubs made this a rewarding day.

In the Great Swamp

I was in the Great Swamp the other Sunday. And as our Sundays usually have been, it was cold and rainy. However, as long as one's feet are soggy wet, it becomes a matter of degree thereafter.

This wetness is a high factor in keeping many people out of the plant hunting business, ranking with Poison Ivy and snakes. Out of the mores of our childhood we have developed a mental block which says that it is impossible to walk in water when shod and clothed. Yet there is nothing more protective than shoes and clothes when wallowing about in this element, and it is just our stodginess that says it cannot be done.

Furthermore, it is a delightful experience as any young child may tell you, soothing and buoyant, the odor of methane and muck is not prolonged, and it is the most effective method of reaching a choice bit of vegetation 20 feet out into a pool. But I doubt many people will ever convert to it, and cars will still stop by the roadside, their occupants to gaze with puzzled amazement at men floundering around in the water. I suppose it does strike the uninitiated as a form of mild insanity. Few people realize how quickly clothes dry when one is moving about in the open air.

I recall the first time I was out botanizing with James Leland Edwards more than 15 years ago. We had come to a stretch of deep water. Without comment or change of course or pace he walked into the water, gradually going deeper to the mid-stream, the water splashing at his armpits, holding his pocket belongings over his head. When he reached the opposite bank he plunged onward, trailing a great stream of water. I was astounded, but could do no less.

Last Summer I saw Bayard Long, a man in his seventies, walk knee- and hip-deep in water all day long, and carrying a heavy collecting case at that. These old-time botanists are a rugged crew.

The Great Swamp is just the last stage of the once huge Lake Passaic which existed as the ice melted some ten or twenty thousand years ago. This old lake bed, rimmed by the Watchungs, comprises the beginnings of the present-day Passaic River. Water is plentiful, the streams run slow and heavy, banks full, and the road bridges just clear the water.

It is not completely swamp and wet. Various areas run to sedge and cattail marshes and wet woods, but the bulk of it is suitable for farming and residential purposes. As in many parts of New Jersey, a large acreage is reverting back to woodland. From the traces of old lanes and fence lines it is likely that all but the actual narrow marshes were once heavily farmed.

In addition to main highways, old roads and paths, now largely overgrown, thread the area so no large section of the Swamp is inaccessible even to the casual hiker. Perhaps the general impression is one of ever-present water nearby, but not the wateriness usually associated with such a name as Great Swamp. It is not as wet, for instance, as the Troy Meadows, a name which implies no water. But then in our own Hunterdon County the area above Hardscrabble and Croton is still called The Swamp.

Water to the botanist means a wholly different series of plants, so the streams were our interest. Specifically, we were looking for Feather-foil, a rare and interesting aquatic plant, and, to dispose of that subject, we did not find it.

At the first stop bladderworts were already in bloom, the intricate yellow flowers thrust above the water on wiry stems. A free-floating liverwort (Riccia natans) was here abundant, just scraps of minute greenery to the wayward eye, and that large alga, a Chara genus sometimes called Stonewort or Muskgrass. Pickerelweed and Spatter-dock with big leaves were already shielding much of the stream surfaces.

We stopped at various bridges, seeing the Water Starwort and the Water Parsnip. One area produced the large, showy corymbs of a viburnum, the Witherod, and two northern plants in the Nodding Trillium and Cuckoo-flower.

Finally, we proceeded to an area near Great Brook where an old road had been abandoned, and we took to walking down this road among the warblers singing in the rain and the Veerys. The white Lance-leaved Violet grew in the ruts and little saplings of Sweet Gum were spreading their starry leaves above them.

Since this is an old glacier bed, the cooler plants still persist. Star Flower was in bloom and we came on a fine stand of Pyrola. Our native Wild Garlic was here, much different from the Field Garlic of Europe which we all know, and native irises and the Wood Lily. The waterier buttercups and parsleys were weedy and solid beds of many types of ferns grew beneath the Pin and Swamp White Oaks.

Actually, in these wet woods there are no plants growing which could not be found in similar situations in our northern counties. But there is an air of quiet charm about them when one realizes that this dark and brooding wood is the close suburb of Madison, Chatham, Summit, and other growing cities.

It is a fascinating area, a little bit of wild Jersey where even the otter may at times be seen. But its greatest allure is the sense of water aplenty, of full and deep streams winding, pulsing thickly, teeming richly with the life of water, throbbing onward to the open bays.

IV

Friends and Foes of Man

Cherries Sour and Sweet

I saw a family the other day busily picking sour cherries from a small tree which grew along the road. These were the familiar red, sour cherries which botanically are called Prunus Cerasus. Yet my thoughts were not so much on the cherry tree, a familiar species which now and then escapes to grow naturally along fence lines, but on the absence these days of cherry picking in June.

Time was when cherry picking became a youngster's occupation in June. Fortunately, it was always one of the pleasanter tasks, since ripe cherries, sweet and pulpy, are good food. It is not so much that times have changed against cherry picking but that there are no cherries to pick.

I have heard that some of the fungus diseases have wiped out the numerous roadside and fence-line cherry trees. More probably their decline comes from a general lack of interest. Many of these cherry trees were planted and then grafted. Few people plant cherry trees any more. Even fewer know how to graft.

These sweet cherries came in many horticultural colors and sizes, red, black, yellow. They were really all one species—Prunus Avium, an old European development. There are many trees of this Sweet Cherry still around but they are reverting to a smaller, less desirable fruit. The birds still like them.

The Sour Cherry and the Sweet Cherry were brought over early by the colonists. The only native cherry of consequence that we have locally is the Rum Cherry, so-called for its frequent use years ago to flavor rum and other spirits.

This wild, black cherry actually is a forest tree but we know it as a weedy thing of roadsides, fence rows, and abandoned fields where it is subject to periodic infestations by the Tent Caterpillar.

When not denuded by caterpillars our Rum Cherry produces heavy crops, but the individual fruits are small so that mostly they are left to the Robins and other birds and only the cuckoos are interested in the Tent Caterpillar crop.

We do have another cherry species through Hunterdon that is somewhat common but few people know it. This is the true Choke Cherry, a northerly tree that we know only as a shrub no more than waist high. It forms small thickets here and there along the roads and in untended fence corners. Its flowering is abundant and showy but it flowers in May when there is so much of other bloom around that it is hardly noticed.

It does not bear sweet fruit, as may be deduced from its name. Rather, the fruit is puckery and acid. Yet it is not altogether unpleasant. And the caterpillars do not bother it nearly so much.

Hunterdon boasts another cherry species but this is more a botanical curiosity than anything else. It is called the Sand Cherry, Prunus depressa. This species is a prostrate, creeping tree which forms round patches up to six feet in diameter on sand or gravel. It has a spectacular bloom and excellent fruit but it is decidedly rare.

There were some plants of this cherry growing along the railroad which follows the Delaware several years ago and it was reported from the banks of the river proper back some 50 years or more ago. Since then the railroad has been spraying its right-of-way to kill off plants and whether it is existent in this county at this writing I do not know.

It has a near relative, called Prunus susquehanae, which is an upright tree or shrub. Both species are supposedly common around the sand dunes of the Great Lakes. We know the susquehanae type only as a small shrub a foot or two in height which leads a precarious existence atop the exposed rocks and ledges of Kittatinny Mountain. It is very rare here, however.

One other cherry completes our New Jersey list of this genus. This is the Fire or Pin Cherry. It is a shrub or small tree of sandy, rocky, or sterile soil. It is more of a mountain tree than the other species and I have never seen it in Hunterdon but perhaps others have. The Pin Cherry has an odd, unround fruit on long stems. It is edible but not pleasant. In New Jersey it is most likely to be found in such areas of exposed rock as where the Appalachian Trail traverses through the state.

Certainly we have enough of cherry species in our state to satisfy the student. But for some of us this is not quite enough, those of us who remember the Oxheart Cherry, for example.

It is not all nostalgia, either. Those old-time cherry trees produced a wonderful, abundant fruit. They produced enough cherries for every family and every boy around and every wandering bird. They produced a crop even for the field mice who harvested the pits for Winter food.

Doubtless, the Sweet Cherry will not return. But then this generation will have something else to remember from its growing-up time. All generations do.

Trees

Has there lived a person who has been unmoved by the sight of a big tree? Most of us may not know the difference between an ash and an oak, but the sight of a forest giant towering skyward brings an immediate reaction of awe and wonder to all.

Unfortunately, the only method known to produce a big tree is to leave it strictly alone and for many years, generally more than one person's lifetime. For the soaring trees of today we must thank the hands and the dreams of those long gone from the living.

The Pitch Pine of southern Jersey is often regarded as one of the scrubbier species by those uninformed of the history of wood in the Pine Barrens. Charcoal burners and bog farmers, timbermen, and careless fires have all contributed to eliminating the Pitch Pine before its prime.

Where it has been undisturbed for at least a century this tree shows a stately magnificence. I saw such a one recently, perhaps the largest Pitch Pine, down in Atlantic County. It grows within a hundred yards of Black Horse Pike on the site of a proposed industrial park.

This tree is close to 12 feet in circumference at breast height. By triangulation it is 97 feet high and it rises some 50 feet from the ground to the first limb. The tree is healthy and still growing.

My course was next to Mays Landing to see native mistletoe in bud. This is a rare plant in New Jersey but it is known to be in at least several spots. Here they are growing on Sour Gum as the plants do in other Jersey localities. It is inclined to favor certain species in specific locales, Sour Gum in one area, maple in another.

Our native chestnut only grows to withe or sapling size before the still present blight finds it. Only a rare tree will produce burrs and that for only a year or two. But down on a little peninsula formed within a curve of the Great Egg Harbor River is a cluster of these trees sufficiently large in size to tell us of this generation what the chestnut looked like. They are not vigorous. They do not grow well. Rather, they are sprawling, appearing as stump growths, but they are almost a foot in diameter and show no immediate damage from the blight. Chestnut burrs are thick beneath them but the squirrels have left only the worm-ridden nuts.

Some Jerseyites claim that the Bald Cypress we visited in Cape May County along Sluice Creek is native. This is more pride than fact and the Bald Cypress just has not been found as native in New Jersey.

For the story of this tree I quote from Robert C. Alexander's *Noteworthy Trees of Cape May County,* written in 1949, "In open woods on north shore of Sluice Creek, South Dennis, west of dam at Clint's Mill. Pointed out to Witmer Stone sometime before 1911 by Henry Walker Hand who mentioned a second cypress that formerly grew downstream toward the bay. Trappers found the tree at Clint's Mill later and, at that time, it was given considerable publicity. This Bald Cypress was probably planted in the 1880s by James van Gilder, a resident at Clint's Mill, who was engaged in the shipping and lumber business in the south. Cir. 7 ft. 4½ in., Ht. 55 ft., Spread 25 ft." *

A further excerpt from Alexander is as follows: "Big Tulip Tree named 'King Nummy' in Timber and Beaver Swamp near Clermont. In 1932, Dr. Julius Way wrote, 'This tree measures 28½ feet around the base and carries a gradually reducing circumference to a height of 65 feet before the branches appear. Although the heart of the tree has decayed away and the top has been blown off, its deeply fluted trunk bids fair to remain intact for many years to come.' The same year, Otway Brown listed the circumference as 19 feet 1 inch three to four feet from the ground. Several years ago, the only sign of life was a sprig of leaves growing near the top of the broken trunk. The present condition is not known to me. One of the largest trees in the county in recent times." †

We managed to get to this tree after a trek of at least one half mile through two feet and more of chilly water. The tree is still much alive and still growing. My companions, the Hirst brothers, triangulate this tree as 117 feet tall. It is tremendous. Its mound as it rises from the brown, swamp water must be 50 feet in circumference.

It stands among other giants in a deep, sphagnum swamp heavy with girthy Sweet and Sour Gums, Red Maple, and holly. Here grow the biggest magnolias and Basket Oaks in the state. The swamp will be drier in Summer, but a guide should be used by those wishing to penetrate its moody interior.

We added one more good tree to our list before the day was done. This was the Pond Pine, a southern relative of the Pitch. We finally ran across it in a fine grove of pines down near Town Bank. Here grows the Pond along with Loblolly, Pitch, and Virginia Pine in a luxuriant stand reminiscent of the high, fertile groves on the Eastern Shore of Maryland and Virginia.

* Robert C. Alexander, *Noteworthy Trees of Cape May County.* Cape May, New Jersey: Cape May Geographic Society, c. 1949, p. 13.
† *Ibid.,* p. 33.

THE BACKYARD WILDERNESS

Amanita Mushrooms

I picked up a mushroom on the roadside down in Brookville Hollow. Up the road apiece Art Christensen was checking his mailbox. I showed it to him.

This was really a good-looking mushroom. It was so unique it did not look like a mushroom and both Art and I marvelled at it. It arose from a hard and bulbous base, pure white and fringed with a white laciness. The cup was globular, not much larger than the bulbous base and not at all spreading like the usual versions of mushroom.

Furthermore, this upper sphere was lacquered in a glossy yellow, a shining yellow that deepened to a living orange at the edges and this all was flecked with bits of material like a sprinkle of shredded coconut. It looked delectable.

Up in Sergeantsville I took it into Venable's Store and someone saw it and asked: "Is that a bowling trophy?" Across the street another man peered at it and guessed that it was a carved chess piece. Only one gentleman came near the truth with the remark that it looked like the mushrooms in the old country that were used to kill flies.

For sure enough this was an Amanita, the Fly Agaric, Amanita muscaria, brilliantly colored, attractive and poisonous, beautiful and deadly.

In the wild, flies and other insects are attracted to it and will sip of the juice on the moist cap. Rings of dead flies surrounding the cap have been found so rapid is its poison. It has been used as an ingredient of fly poisons for centuries.

There are four typical Amanitas in our range. Two are non-poisonous, the Orange Amanita or Royal Agaric and the Blushing Venenarius. The two poisonous ones, the Destroying Angel and the Fly Poison, are perhaps the deadliest of all mushrooms. The poisonous property in the Amanitas is muscarin.

They all are listed as common. While not a mushroom enthusiast I do keep my eyes open and I find all Amanitas uncommon in Hunterdon County. This was the first time I had ever seen the Fly Poison.

I have heard it said that all mushrooms are edible and all toadstools are poisonous. Let me clear this up. Toadstools are just another name for types of mushrooms and the name has no bearing on edibility. The poisonous mushrooms must be learned one by one. In addition, testing for the discoloration of a silver coin or spoon means nothing, or the lack of discoloration, while in preparation for the table. Believe this not.

Since the mushrooms that are edible are so delicious it is unfortunate that many are so deadly. Most people can recognize the family Agaricus growing in the field and know it to be edible since it is also the store-bought mushroom yet there is an impressive series of various mushrooms all having tastes and qualities all their own. But since most of us will hesitate to trust our own identification we had better trust to the grocery stores.

There comes to mind a rather distinguished mycologist who does his field work equipped with a frying pan and some butter. In the woods when he chances on a particularly delectable species he promptly kindles a little fire and feasts on freshly fried mushrooms. It is said that the tastiness of mushrooms are at their height at the moment of picking.

This does save carrying food, always a bother, while hiking through the woods. People solve this problem in various ways. I recall the story told of one of our noted lichenologists who goes afield with a big box of crackers to stave off the hunger pangs. He also uses the cracker box to hold his lichen specimens, gathering lichens and nibbling crackers all day. But he is afflicted with a certain amount of absent-mindedness and there are trips wherein by the end of the day he has eaten up most of his lichen specimens along with the crackers.

I have seen field groups so loaded down with food cartons and Thermos jugs that nothing was ever accomplished during the day through this great concern for the stomach. Generally, the more seasoned field men travel light.

One old-time Jersey ornithologist long since gone carried this to the extreme. He took no food at all on field trips. He stated that most groups carried too much food anyway and he was doing them a favor in taking some off their hands at noon. Also, he maintained he achieved a varied and healthful diet by reason of this random sampling.

But I think the mushroom hunters have it best of all—a frying pan and a little butter and like gods they can feast on the savory mushrooms.

A Great Big Pain in the Neck

Blackbird is a general term as nonspecific as the words rodent, duck, or oak. In the sense of defining something, it means nothing.

In New Jersey we have several birds that are blackish. We have none

Amanita muscaria

that is entirely black. The individual species run from rare to abundant. Certainly such birds as Brewer's Blackbird or the Yellow-headed Blackbird, which are mere accidental vagrants from the mid-west, cannot be classed as adverse economic factors in food crops such as sweet corn.

The huge Boat-tailed Grackle of our southern states has a colony along Delaware Bay but it cannot be seen more than a few hundred yards from tidewater. The Rusty Blackbird that usually travels with Robins in Spring and Fall is so scarce that even good bird observers are unfamiliar with it.

Cowbirds that have been hatched and reared by Song Sparrows and Yellow Warblers have now found their brethren and small flocks are on the wheat stubble. But through the curious arrangement of their perpetuation Cowbirds can never be a plague to anyone.

Years ago the Bobolink of the Timothy fields of New England was a nuisance in the rice fields of the Carolinas in Autumn, but the rice fields have gone and reed birds are no longer a problem.

This leaves us with two aggressive species which could be of interest to our south Jersey farmers. The Red-winged Blackbird has expanded from the salt marshes to breed commonly everywhere in the grass fields. The Purple Grackle has thrived mightily as a direct result of the suburbanite's bounty. In all the Norway Spruces, the Austrian Pines, and other evergreens planted so extravagantly about our homes in town and country it has found a virtual paradise.

It loves the thick evergreens. In Hunterdon County, beyond a few minor groups still using the dwindling Osage Orange hedges, they have moved exclusively into the evergreen plantings, and with the current fancy of planting our old fields to cheap pine and spruce the Purple Grackle will continue to prosper.

This is just another example of the self-defeat we encounter when we attempt to reorganize Nature. In this instance we find one type of farming in indirect conflict with another.

The world of the wild is always well in balance, a condition achieved over the millenia of time. If nothing out of doors is disturbed there will be no change in the status of growing and living things. But change or disturbance brings forth wide counterchange and parallel disturbance. Additions or deletions in habitat of flora or fauna automatically produce tremendous lists of additions and deletions up and down the scale of other flora and fauna. For every action there is reaction —still a basic, simple law of Nature.

But Nature can be slow in the eyes of one generation alone. When the Starling was introduced the counterbalance of disease, parasite, and predator on the Starling was not also introduced, therefore the Starling runs rampant over the land.

The Japanese Honeysuckle is not a pest in Japan and the Starling is not a menace in Europe. The balances have been achieved. A few score years in North America have not given natural controls time in which to develop for either. We cannot import a selective disease upon the Starling, as was done to control the Japanese Beetle, or even a selective parasite.

At the present time, the Starling must be defined as an introduced parasite on man in the class of the House Fly, Norway Rat, and any controls must be in the immediate environment of man's living. We must not forget that in general terms man in North America is also an introduced species unadjusted and as an introduced species man has caused great disruption.

In all probability, the bulk of the blackbird trouble is only Starling trouble. The hordes are over the countryside. Noisy and brash, they invade the deep city. They usurp the salt marsh to frustrate the tiny, timid Black Rail. They eat the sweet corn and they sneak past the gulls to steal clams on the beaches.

They befoul the cherries and the blueberries. They drive the Wood Thrush from the Dogwood berries. They muss up state capitols as well as crossroad settlements. They are everywhere and everywhere they are a great big pain in the neck.

Owls

Otto Heck came by the other evening to tell me that he had found another Great Horned Owl's nest near where I live. He asked me if I would like to see it.

Off we went in the late afternoon to a remote part of Delaware Township to look at the nest. Otto said it was right near the road, but after wading through several fields and a number of thickets, I wondered about his use of qualifying words.

After a few ditches we entered a noble wood. The beeches soared and the oaks towered. Here was one of those few woods which had escaped the periodic lumbering so characteristic of Hunterdon County. It was a noble wood of forest giants.

We stopped about 200 feet short of the nest. It was high up in an ancient Pignut Hickory. Clearly outlined against the sky were the two young ones peering intently at us with all the fierce alertness of their family.

We went no farther for fear of alarming the parents who would be close by watching us, but hidden from our eyes. We quietly left the vicinity with the owl eyes still fixed upon us. Judging from their size, the young were almost ready to leave the nest.

As he does every year, Otto has discovered a large number of owl nests, proving that this family is well represented in Hunterdon during the breeding season. His specialty at the time was the Longeared Owl. He had several nests under observation that Spring. He has located a number of Sawwhet Owls which spend the Winter here, but he has yet to find a Sawwhet Owl nest.

Otto Heck has observed a number of paired Red-tailed Hawks in western Hunterdon which indicates a high breeding population of this bulky, slow-moving rodent hawk. Years ago this raptor was a rarity in Summer but its numbers as a breeder have increased tremendously in the past decade.

Conversely, the Red-shouldered Hawk has dropped in number. Along with the Broad-winged it was our common breeding buteonine hawk but today it is quite rare. Perhaps the increase in both the acreage of woodlands and their size has not been suited to their needs.

Thyme and Other Plants

The attractions in our plant world are many. Beyond such utilitarian stuff as lumber, fiber, and grain, the prosaic food, clothing, and shelter aspect of plants are further worlds.

It could be the world of wine and honey, ambrosial to the senses, or it might be one of gentler allurement. From many an herb of wood or plant of field might be unrolled a chronicle of legend and lore, a thing of time-misty fable and old history.

In the consideration of shrub and blossom are limitless associations. These could be Biblical or historical, Shakespearean or Elizabethan, fact or fancy.

There is a pleasure in forgotten herbals and officinals, in the simple plants of garden that flowered and perfumed the air our ancestors breathed and withal then made lively names for them. In our plants is our history and our life.

VINCENT ABRAITYS

Surely we have a pleasurable heritage in these charming names. Rosemary and Basil, Lavender and Marjoram, rich, redolent sounds, Cicely and Thyme, Hyssop and Germander, sweet to taste. Tarragon, Pennyroyal, Lad's Love, and Chamomile, all heady.

History, fable, and legend give no plant richer endowment than the lowly Thyme. Already old and honored in ancient Greece, it has intrigued the roll of generations since. It is a creeping little herb but be it in wine or honey, incense or poet's rhyme, the aromatic shrub retains mysterious allure.

Mathews prosaicly says: "A European, rather weedy plant closely related to cultivated thyme, but usually cultivated only for ornament, from which it escapes in many parts of our range . . . It generally escapes into woods and fields." *

That it should have escaped our colonial gardens was inevitable. That it is not at all abundant, even scarce, is the pity.

My own experience with the plant has been poor. Several years ago I chanced on a single stem of Wild Thyme along the Garden State Parkway down in Atlantic County. It was probably introduced as an impurity in the seedings of the road bank and would not long persist. A single plant is no bank of Wild Thyme glowing in the sun.

However some things have come to pass and now I have seen a bank in bloom. I concur with the perceptive Greeks. A bank of Wild Thyme in full bloom is lovely beyond words.

It was up in Sussex County and along an obscure farm road. The plant had taken over a dry shale bank where nothing else would grow and so it presented a close and solid pile to the sun, very dense but only a few inches high. It was in full blossom of a likeness of Moss Pink but with a nature all its own. It was a solid rose-pink bank. Perhaps no perfume arose from it but I thought my throat was caught in the odor of Wild Thyme.

Here on the piedmont we had in abundance the Red Cedar which is really a juniper. Near to the Wild Thyme was an old pasture which had been invaded by Common Juniper, which is a juniper that looks like a juniper.

It had some of the qualities of Ground Juniper, that is, a depressed state of growth since it was clumpy and spreading-branched almost like a lawn ornamental. It dotted in dark mounds across the worn-out pasture.

On crossing to the juniper clumps along the way was a stand of Hoary Alyssum. Here is a comparatively recent addition to North

---

* F. Schuyler Mathews, *Field Book of American Wild Flowers*, revised and enlarged by Norman Taylor. New York: G. P. Putnam's Sons, 1955, p. 430.

THE BACKYARD WILDERNESS

America flora. Our botanists of a past generation did not know it.

Benner's *The Flora of Bucks County, Pennsylvania,** which was issued in 1932, does not mention it and Tatnall's *Flora of Delaware and the Eastern Shore* †, published as late as 1946, does not record it either. My first notation on the plant was in 1958 in the vicinity of Centerville on the Somerset County line. In 1961 and 1962 it appeared to be increasing on the hills around Teetertown and Little Brook.

Along the fence near the junipers was a cropped-over patch of the golden-flowered Our Lady's Bedstraw, reputed to be the true bedstraw used in the manger at Bethlehem. Its thin, woody stems showed the whorled leafing of all the bedstraws. Also at a little distance I saw a minty clump that was Wild Marjoram in bud, which seems to prefer this colder habitat in from the sea, for it is abundant on the roadsides of upper Sussex County. With many plants only the space of a few miles separates scarcity from abundance.

The latitudes of growth of many European introductions approximates pretty much their growth areas in Europe. This is why so many of these plants reach their best growth as we travel northward into New York State and New England, and the Provinces of Quebec and New Brunswick.

So here on a sterile ridge of shale in Sussex County, against the darkness of juniper and budding Marjoram, were such colors as the white of Hoary Alyssum and the fading gold of bedstraw along with the pink charm of Wild Thyme.

Perhaps I shall be fortunate to pass this way again.

Bats

This is a good year for bats. Several are harboring somewhere in the eaves of my home and a number of other people are playing host to them. A friend tells me that they are in especial quantity around Croton, New Jersey.

---

* Walter M. Benner, *The Flora of Bucks County, Pennsylvania*. Philadelphia: published by the author, 1932.
† Robert R. Tatnall, *Flora of Delaware and the Eastern Shore: An Annotated List of the Ferns and Flowering Plants of the Peninsula of Delaware, Maryland, and Virginia.* Dover, Delaware (?): The Society of Natural History of Delaware, 1946.

VINCENT ABRAITYS

Mostly, bats are unobtrusive mammals. Only when one of them miscalculates his exits and winds up in the living room are they ever of concern to people. Only in these circumstances do most people observe them.

This is perhaps good since so much sinister but untrue legend surrounds them. The small creatures, furthermore, are faced today with the propaganda that some have been found afflicted with rabies. If true, obviously the proportion must be small and since any mammal may become rabid, bats are no more dangerous.

Few but the most careful observers note the always large number of bats around. One of my correspondents says they are quite abundant in his Round Valley area. In that vicinity they would frequent the limestone caves that now and then get in the news.

In late Summer bats scatter from their breeding grounds, as do birds, and begin a slight southward movement. They are reputed to hibernate through Winter but there appears to be a difinite migration. This may take them a slight distance southward in the late Summer. It is in this season that they are most often seen garnering their food in early twilight.

I recall several years ago in early Spring along the Kittatinny an acquaintance from Lebanon was scaling bark from old trees in his quest for moths. Behind a chunk of dead bark he found a bat crouched tightly waiting out the daylight hours beneath the dark safety of the bark.

They can be found in old buildings, attics, belfries, silos, barns, hollow trees, and caves. Caves have always held an attraction for bats and they had located all of them long before such a term as speleology was coined.

Bats are placed in a grouping that is named Chiroptera by the mammalogist. In this group are several families or sub-groupings so that in our area the eight representatives of Chiroptera are either bats, pipistrelles, or myotis. Unless one is a student the differences between them are really not important and we may well call them all bats.

The Little Brown Myotis is probably the bat we see most often flying near water in the dusk, and the bat most often seen at sundown around houses while there is still some light is the Eastern Pipistrelle. Both the Red Bat and the Big Brown Bat are regular throughout this range. These are larger bats but in casual observation the size is not a field characteristic. Only on September evenings, when many bats are moving, can the eye note that several sizes of bats are passing by.

Four other bats occur in our range, the Keen Myotis and the Small-footed Myotis, the Silver-haired Bat and the Hoary Bat. The two myotis are distinguished by technical standards only from the very

Little Brown Myotis

common Little Brown Myotis. Both the Silver-haired Bat and the Hoary Bat are rare and are to be found only in forested regions. Generally, they are solitary bats who by preference do not mingle with others of their kind.

Howard Drinkwater tells me that once he was brought a Hoary Bat for identification and Lee Edwards has one record for New Jersey. But most naturalists do not concern themselves with bats. Bat knowledge is a specialty item and no one of my acquaintance is versed in their ways and their kinds. The story of this retiring mammal involves the disagreeable task of crawling in and out of caves and up in the eaves and gables of buildings.

Since bats fly only at night and are completely secretive in their ways specimens are always needed for accurate identification. In this respect they are completely different from birds who move by day and are visible, who sing and are heard.

It is assumed that bats are subject to the same risks of living that confront all living things. While our bats are strictly insectivorous certainly other animal life preys upon them. In their sleeping quarters they would be exposed to the cat family and the mustelines, to snakes, and all manner of predacious beings. In flight they can be caught by any member of the owl family. In early evening they are exposed to hawks.

Nonetheless, in their world they have found a secure niche safe from the prying eyes of man and theirs is the least explored terrain. Their contact with man remains completely innocuous.

Our bats are interested only in securing sufficient insect life from the night air to keep body together and propagate their kind. While there are some of us who may be interested in bats, it is doubtful if the bats are at all concerned with man.

Mulleins and Herbicides

The delicate steeples of Moth Mullein are flowering now in the waste places and along the roadsides. Daily the flowers mount the spires.

The Moth Mullein is another of those charming imports from Europe whose ancestry is now unknown. I conjecture that its name alludes to its attractiveness for various moths. I find no other reason for its name and, strangely, no medicinal uses. It achieves a modest two or three feet of height but it has a long blooming period since the flowers open individually as the plant grows upward. The flowers open out horizontally and thus are completely visible to the eye.

Ordinarily, the flowers are yellow with lavenderish centers but now and then a white form appears. It is merely a color aberration and both kinds may be found growing together as they are in a field at the north end of Frenchtown where this June they are putting on a particularly fine display.

All of us have noticed later in the year the Giant Mullein with its yellow flowers and fuzzy leaves. The stalks of this species are so rigid they tend to remain throughout the Winter.

A specialty plant of the Delaware River bottoms is another mullein, the White Mullein, which is now beginning to bloom. It is a pleasant looking plant but it occurs in too limited a range to be appreciated by many.

There are two other mullein species in our eastern states. All five act as if they were native but, truthfully, all are immigrants. However they have so adapted themselves here that it is doubtful they will be ever eliminated.

Lebanon Township was one of the few Hunterdon County municipalities to spray its roadsides with weed killer. Happily it has discontinued the practice.

Weed killers are not selective. What is poisonous to one life form is invariably poisonous to all life forms and all life forms suffer when herbicides and insecticides are applied.

I have a particular interest in the Lebanon Township case since in the late 1950s I noted an interesting plant growing on the roadbank near Anthony. This was the Mole Spurge or Caper Plant. I suppose this plant had escaped from some old garden nearby. It was rather a handsome plant and it was cultivated for medicinal uses besides, although the euphorbias are notorious for their poisonous properties.

Two years after I noted the plant the roads were sprayed and one year's spraying destroyed the entire stand. I have never seen the Mole Spurge growing wild anywhere in New Jersey since.

I know that many people will remark with a cynical so what? After all, how many people realized that the plant was there and of what use was it? Nonetheless, mankind is faced with a future which will need to determine whether it can afford to extinguish any more forms of life, animal, or plant.

But I emphasize this fact. What is bad for one growth form is bad for all growth forms and herbicides on the roadbanks are as dangerously pollutant to man as is any other poison which gets into the food chain or is ingested in any other way.

THE BACKYARD WILDERNESS

Snakes!

There was a lively discussion going on in Delaware Township the other evening with regard to snakes. This subject is always long on interest and short on reason, for there is something about our writhing, legless friends that makes women scream, strong men quail, but delights small boys.

It began with the statement that a water moccasin had been killed. I raised the objection that the name was improper, and apt to alarm people needlessly, since so many would assume that this was the Cottonmouth, a poisonous relative of the Copperhead, which does not come far above the Dismal Swamp area of Virginia.

Our snakes of the family Natrix should be called water snakes and nothing more. While vicious and nasty tempered, they are harmless to man even though they are perhaps the most abundant snake of the county. They spend their Summers eating frogs and frightening bathers on every water course of the countryside. Because of their patterned red-browns, this is the snake most often confused with the Copperhead.

Our particular discussion continued until the chopped "water moccasin" was brought in for proof. It was a Milk Snake. This one was killed while going under a barn and was bent on no greater harm than a convenient rat. Along with the Black Snake, the Milk Snake is our most beneficial reptile, our little greenish Garter Snake being equipped for no more than grasshoppers, earthworms, or perhaps a small mouse.

Actually, land snakes in this area are relatively infrequent. All carnivorous animals take them for food as do our Broad-winged Hawks and all our owls. Lately the automobile has been responsible for the major kills and each Spring in the vicinity of the dens in the red shale districts the mortality rate of the Black Snake is high.

One of the least seen yet common snakes is our Copperhead, which thrives well in Hunterdon County. Generally nocturnal, it tries to spend its days under a log, beneath a stone, or entwined on the base of some shrub. We seem to be fairly consistent in producing about one Copperhead bite per year in the county, none of which have been fatal to my knowledge.

The Copperhead emerges from its Winter den sometime in early Spring. This den will be some inconspicuous crevice or fissure in stone leading deep enough to be frostless in Winter. To be dry, it will be fairly high up some rocky hillside, and it will face east or south to catch the rising sun. It will have honeysuckle, grapevine, or shrubs about to afford concealment as the sluggish snakes pick up warmth in April.

As the days grow longer and the heat increases, the snakes will move farther from the den so that by July none will be around it. Heat increases their activity and their food demands, and they forage afield till about mid-August when they will have reached their extreme limit of range. Then the reports come in of Copperheads in hayfields, gardens, and woods. The average range is about two miles. As the days wane the snakes work back to the rocks of their hillsides. More and more time is now spent in the den until there will be a day in October when the Copperhead takes his last look at the falling leaves and retires for the Winter.

My last encounter with a Copperhead to advantage was in the early part of September of last year on an unfrequented ridge in Sussex County below Port Jervis. David Fables and I were botanizing this little known, rugged area on a hot, humid day, and we were crossing a series of hogback limestone outcrops high above the Delaware. I was in the lead paralleling a strip of vegetation growing in a narrow seam of the otherwise barren rock when I heard a faint rustling, and I stopped.

The Copperhead was undoubtedly moving back to his den and hearing us had halted in anticipation. Calmly and unconcernedly he poised there at our feet. He must have shed just recently for in the sunlight he shone and glowed in gleaming coppers. Truly, he was beautiful. We circled him and although he looked larger, a careful estimate of his length was only 38 inches. We surveyed each other with interest at some length, and then the snake, in the urgency of latening time, moved slowly and purposefully down the ridge.

Over the years there has been an occasional reliable report of rattlers along the Musconetcong highlands. These probably represent only cyclic attempts at range extensions, for in the more northern counties the Timber Rattlesnake is barely holding his own. Even rarer is the rattler of southern Jersey whose stronghold, if any, has been in the Mount Misery area, although reported from many other spots. This snake will den in sand under the roots of fallen trees. Few people, including the writer, have ever seen one, and it is thought that it is more closely related to the Canebrake Rattlesnake of the south than the Timber Rattler of the mountains.

But however interesting the snakes of New Jersey may be, I doubt that man will suddenly develop great love for them, and I am sure they will continue to be killed on sight and run down by cars on the roads. I am equally sure they will not become extinct.

Hawks, Swifts, and Monarch Butterflies

The first Nighthawks of the Autumn season came over on the early afternoon of Labor Day in that lazy, flip-flop way of their kind, so like big butterflies. Nighthawks are so large that it is difficult to believe tiny insects compose their entire diet.

It is not unusual to have Nighthawks pass through at this time of year. It would be unusual if they did not.

But along with the Nighthawks there came many Chimney Swifts. Nighthawks and Chimney Swifts all came from the northeast and held a course to the southwest, which is the classic migrational route over this area of our country.

The swifts came into view and passed on continually and I realized that I was seeing hundreds of swifts and that this was a heavy wave of traveling birds.

Interspersed among the swifts were many of the swallow family —Tree Swallows, Bank Swallows, and Barn Swallows. While watching the smaller birds pass by I noticed two Turkey Vultures so high in the sky that they were mere specks. They also were sailing southwestward on set wings in the accepted manner of migrating vultures.

The little wind that was blowing came from the south and the sky was beginning to haze. A weather change could be felt in the air. It was logical to assume that the falling barometer, an onset of bad weather, had triggered off a definite migrational wave in the area, and obeying certain instincts the birds were hastening to leave an area which was to experience a storm.

The why and how of migrating birds is still pretty much in the air. We are apt to say that a cold front brings in the birds and it does, but when we say it that way the conclusion becomes that an onset of high pressure is the triggering impulse to bird migration. This should not be the implication or conclusion at all. I feel that closer study will show that a falling barometer is the migrational stimulus and a rising barometer grounds the birds. Bad weather starts the migration, good weather halts it. This appears to hold true in the Fall.

The halting of the migration after a high moves in is why we see birds after the cold front moves in from the west or northwest and passes to the east. The high pressure did not bring them in, the low pressure did. The good weather stalled the birds.

Up at Hawk Mountain they have a saying that a good hawk flight appears a day or two after a severe storm in New England.

This is correct. However, there is an implication that bad weather has caused the birds to leave and that they will travel in the good weather and the hawk flights only occur in good weather.

Apparently this is not correct. What is seen at Hawk Mountain on those first blustery days after a cold front has moved in from the west is not the beginning of a hawk flight but the termination of it.

The passage of birds at Hawk Mountain is purely fortuitous. It could even be termed accidental. Those birds that are still in flight from the low pressure storms invariably begin to encounter strong head winds from the advancing high pressure cell. There is a tendency to advance against these winds while the migrational stimulus still remains.

At any ridge in a strong wind there is a considerable updraft. Those birds who still retain the dwindling flight stimulus promptly take advantage of the nearest ridge to ease their burden of travel. Therefore Hawk Mountain.

It is coincidence only that sees the flight drop off at Hawk Mountain when the wind stops. The wind stops when the air cell moves in overhead, but the birds have stopped flying anyhow because of the good weather.

Admittedly all of this is theory but I feel it answers more of the questions of flight and migration than many of the other theories in print.

While watching for hawks on the Kittatinny recently several Monarch Butterflies went past. They came out of the north and flew to the south despite a quartering wind.

They were fragile bits of matter, scraps before the wind it seemed, ready to be torn by its violence and cast down like the dry leaves that whirled around them.

Yet they were not torn apart by the wind. They persisted before the wind and they flew ever southward in a relentless endeavor. Each year the Monarchs fly over the ridges. They are most abundant in September but they are still common in October and some are seen in November.

They migrate on a broad front. Earlier in the Fall I was in Cape May and along the beaches the Monarch Butterflies clustered thickly on the Seaside Goldenrod. They appeared to rest here before the long flight across Delaware Bay.

THE BACKYARD WILDERNESS

While they were flying here they were flying a thousand miles southward. William Ward wrote to me from Lawrenceville, Georgia: "Monarch Butterflies passing over here for better than a week now. Probably 20 or more an hour at a given point, headed southwest, mostly singles with a few pairs."

It is logical to assume then that the distance between New Jersey and Georgia at least was filled with Monarchs migrating south. This makes for a tremendous number.

Not only is the Monarch an intrepid navigator and traveler, he is a valiant battler. Of course he tastes so terrible that no bird will eat him but he has such a nasty temper that there are many recorded instances where he has pursued Kingbirds. He fears nothing.

Up in Canada this year there was quite a project of banding Monarchs. Small clips visible at a distance were set in the insect's wings. I did not see any banded butterflies but one gentleman I encountered who made a specialty of this told me he saw three.

Presumably the Monarch Butterfly migrates to the Gulf Coast where it spends the Winter. In Spring it begins to move northward, breeding as it comes. The wasted, older ones die out but the young continue the flight northward. Several generations later, in mid-Summer, they have reached Canada where they again begin the long flight southward.

During a recent hot spell I watched a Monarch Butterfly still depositing eggs in New Jersey while all around were others of its kind moving southwestward.

Would the larvae still have time to hatch and pupate? Perhaps. Don Adelberg of Johnsonburg in Warren County tells me that the Monarch Butterfly can go through the growing state in a period of about a week that takes other butterflies up to six weeks. In a warm Fall the eggs which I saw deposited can hatch and go through the cycle of adulthood and still take off for the south.

The act of depositing eggs was puzzling to watch, puzzling because as far as I was concerned the butterfly either knew her terrain and knew where the individual milkweed plants were growing or else had an instantaneous recognition of milkweeds from some distance. The female flew in an almost straight line, dipping swiftly and lightly to plant a single egg on a single leaf.

Since the Monarch was traveling at what I felt was near top speed, the act of dipping and laying almost in flight was incomprehensible to me. How did the insect recognize the milkweed?

I posed this question to Adelberg but he had no solution. He surmised that the insect used some special sense, probably through ultra-violet radiation or chemo-receptive mechanisms, to spot her plants.

At any rate, the Monarch knew its task in life. From the number of Monarchs in flight the species was successful about its life duties and would be as long as milkweeds grow.

An Enormous Wasp

Those of the insects who depend on moisture and nectar for their lives have been having a hard time of it this year.

There is a pear tree here, one of those sweet and juicy pears of French ancestry which always bear too much and whose fruit will not keep. It has been dropping pears for a month. Wasps, bees, yellow jackets, hornets, and other unidentified insects have been drinking of the sweet juice. It looks as if the wasp and hornet family have completed their season's cycle since their numbers have gone down since late August.

The honey bees make up the largest segment of the insects at the pears. Since the asters and the goldenrods are just about nonexistent they are forced to these fruit sugars which unfortunately are poor substitutes for the flower nectars which they are able to convert into acceptable sugars. However, the water content is high in this fruit and it certainly assists the hive to exist.

Next in number are the yellow jackets. This is the small bee which nests underground and stings like a fury. This insect and the bumble bee, a few of which are also still on the pears, are the favorite food of skunks. Since the bulk of the colony will die during the Winter those that the skunks take could be termed expendable.

What I want to tell about, though, is not the bumble bee, the honey bee, or others, but a rather rare type of wasp which is here in abundance.

I do not think this wasp is really rare. It is supposed to be widely distributed, but not in number. In the past I have only seen it one at a time. It is an enormous wasp, twice the size of any other, and much bigger than a hornet or bumble bee. It is beautifully colored in dark red and yellow and looks absolutely ferocious.

I have been stung over the years, both as a growing farm boy and as a meddler in the lives of the various things of the wild about me, by just about every stinging bee, wasp, hornet, or whatever but have never been stung by one of these giant wasps. I have no stomach for experimenting with them. They are big. In collecting a couple of specimens I have noted that the amount of poison they exude is considerable and I am sure it is powerful. I speculate on its effects. Has anyone among my readers been hit by one of these out-sized, golden wasps? What's it like?

The name of this wasp is Cicada Killer. It takes the Cicadas that we hear in mid-Summer, which we call locusts hereabouts. These locusts are big so you can imagine how big and powerful these wasps must be to immobilize and then fly away with that large load.

I recall seeing one take a Cicada years ago and it performed a highly efficient job. I'll bet that sting is out of this world. I propose to let the wasp that is called the Cicada Killer alone.

·V·

From North to South

Birds of the Far North

October has been the taste of apples. Hickory nuts have broken from the husk. They gleam whitely now on the fallen hickory leaves. Wood grouse have found Black Haws. Each day the geese fly overhead. They fly in family groups, an orderly line of eight or ten silently, decisively moving southward, or in majestic wedges groping heavily on the sky and their trumpetings turn the eye skyward. The ducks have come and the loons and gannet. The north is growing empty.

Inhospitable to man, the boreal regions are the reservoirs of the bird life of the world. Of all living things only the birds who may come to it quickly and leave with equal winged speed have been able to utilize to fullness the bleak vastness of arctic regions.

These liquid wastes of frozen water and icy pools, of endless tide flats and never-ending flat tundras quaking and oozing under the midnight sun of Summer have brought forth from times uncountable the countless hosts which wing down over the continents.

So too the equally bleak rock lands of the north are blanketed with birds in Summer. The number of fowl that breed upon the rock islands of the Arctic, upon its cold cliffs and promontories, its wet skerries, are inconceivable to us here in the temperate zones, and everywhere strewn are the eggs they lay and the young they bring forth.

Bird islands and bird-egg islands and feather-gathering islands, cliffs and strands abound in northern waters. They have been known since the dawn of man and the succeeding ages of man have preyed upon this vast assemblage for the eggs, the feathers, the meat, the hide, the bones of birds.

This area begins as far south as the coast of Maine and goes up the Gaspé and along the Labradoran headlands through the fiords of Greenland and Iceland, swinging over to Spitzbergen and the myriad islands off the northwest coast of Europe from the Lofoten and Vesteralen though the Faeroes and Hebrides and the Irish coast.

The Eskimos still catch the little Dovekies in hand nets but the barrels of birds for the markets of the world are gone. The down of the eiders is no longer a major article of commerce and it is only in recent times that the gathering of eggs by the shipload has ceased.

Perhaps St. Brendan sailed to the westerly isles and perhaps he did not, but the ancient Celts and Norse have been upon these seas beyond the historian's ken. Once the Labrador Duck visited off the coast of New Jersey and the Great Auk swam in New York's harbor; the down of ducks and alcids clothed these nameless seafarers and the taste of fresh eggs was good to them and the rich, oily meat warming in the cold fogs.

Frederick II of the Holy Roman Empire, one of the more enlightened monarchs of the time, who was born in 1194, wrote a treatise on falconry, *De Arte Venandi cum Avibus*, in which he assembled a wealth of ornithological material beyond his specific subject and where he treated the Greenland falcons, those splendid white falcons pale as the snow who patrol the glittering ice and misty banks of the Arctic. Since this Gyrfalcon could not be found in Europe, it proves the intimate knowledge central Europe possessed of these far-off lands at this date.

That Columbus' highly publicized sight of new lands was the aftermath of a thousand-year knowledge of the coasts of the North Atlantic and North America is generally established.

In the fine sagas of Leif and Karlsefni is a wealth of material alluding to the wild life of Vinland. Wild wheat is mentioned and salmon and the eiders that nested in the usual plenty so that it was difficult to find a way among the eggs.

The weight of evidence to date seems to place Vinland on the Massachusetts coast with the existence there of a colony for perhaps two centuries. However the inclusion of the item on eiders would appear to preclude the Cape Cod area since none of the eiders nest further south than the coast of Maine. Be that as it may, the Vikings of North America lived well where the eiders were.

And perhaps those that left the lands wherein their fathers dwelled achieved in time a harmony of life, to ultimately leave for pleasanter fields.

West Virginia

Dolly Sods was on our itinerary, so that I read with great interest the article in the *New York Times* of July 8, 1973, of one man's visit to this unique area of West Virginia.

The *Times* article was somewhat less than complimentary to both the area and the highway system of the Monongahela National Forest

THE BACKYARD WILDERNESS

on this portion of the Allegheny Mountains. Our visit two days later gave us a completely different viewpoint.

First of all, an ascent or descent of the Allegheny Front is a memorable experience. This huge mountain block, even though it is set among a series of mountains, commands respect. It is the mountain among the many mountains.

It is the Front that has the most awesome of chasms, the steepest of slopes, and the poorest of roads which appear to barely cling to the precipitous sides. It is also the most fascinating and the most beautiful of the mountains, and the area of Dolly Sods is only one of the many scenic and odd botanical areas which the traveler may visit.

The Allegheny Mountain Plateau is a vast plain atop the mountain system which runs recognizably from central Pennsylvania through Maryland into a number of central West Virginia counties. Flat as it is it becomes a windy land, cold and airy in its upper sections, but humid and draped in clouds for much of the time as it increases in altitude in its southern reaches.

It is good farmland in most of its Pennsylvania section but as the plain develops southward it becomes rockier and narrows until in central West Virginia its use is confined to Summer grazing of cattle in the flatter and more accessible portions.

Dolly Sods is a stony area which contains patches of Allegheny Fly-back or Moon-shine Grass, which is a fine feed for livestock despite that when we see it in New Jersey we call it Poverty Grass.

On these Allegheny Fly-back plains are groves of Red Spruce, their branches like pennants turned to the southeast away from the violent and continual northwest winds. With the spruce are the many plants which we know in our northerly areas but which are found here only at the 4,000-foot level and above.

Mountain Ash and the blueberries Laport and I knew, but we were amazed at the sight of the Wild Bleeding Heart, which is also called Turkey Corn and Stagger Weed. Among the boulders and ledges it ran in a deep red riot. I saw the Bleeding Heart again on the summit of Spruce Knob where it colored the rocky top of West Virginia, undaunted by the winds.

Close to Dolly Sods are other flat areas of the same nature. Some have been named so that the map carries designations such as Roaring Plains, Flatrock Plains, and others. All of these summit areas, whether they are called balds, plains, orchards, heaths, or barrens draped in fog and cloud, as they often are, fascinate the eye and hold the senses in their uniqueness.

At another time I visited Gaudineer's Knob. This area contains a portion of the original Red Spruce forest in addition to birch and other hardwoods. The towering trees were all one could imagine of the virgin forests that once clothed these ridges. On the forest road to the Knob there was a hen turkey with two young who scattered excitedly at my approach.

However, plans for this trip were not scenic. It was strictly a botanical venture and the views and panorama were just so much icing on the cake. We were after shale barrens plants, plants which are endemic to certain mountain ridges. These specific ridges are composed of a mid-Devonian age shale that scales and slides and holds little moisture. Over the ages some species of plants have learned to live with these conditions and are not found among other kinds of soil.

We found some shale barrens in Fulton County, Pennsylvania, and traced other outcroppings down through eastern West Virginia. We found some rich, damp hardwood coves on the westerly slopes of the Appalachians in central West Virginia and here we saw species which we do not have in New Jersey.

Yet most impressive was the traverse of the ponderous bulk of the Allegheny Mountains and its lonesome ridges. In the great valleys, in the coves, up lonesomer hollows perhaps was a different West Virginia, one of hardscrabble sustenance, of Pennyroyal tea and the hard culture of mountains, but for me the roll of mountain peaks and the lure of strange plants was sufficient.

Labrador

From where I sat the scene of the sea was of white and a lovely green and the blue of a June morning. It reminded me of the Florida Keys where the white is of the coral and the shades of green and blue in the waters is its depth against the white marl.

But this was Labrador and I was sitting on a lichened rock looking at a disconsolate sea. It was July 15th and the whites were of icebergs and ice chunks floating down the Straits of Belle Isle. And the blues, the lovely blues of a June morn was in the ice projecting up from underground ledges of ice over which the water was of a lovely green.

It was beautiful and somehow deadly looking and most disquieting. It was all disconcerting and disturbing and I had a feeling of a vague uneasiness. Somehow I felt this was no place for a Jerseyman who had left 90 degree heat just a few days previously.

THE BACKYARD WILDERNESS

It was all real enough. The rock ledges of Labrador came down to the sea and the beaches were of scree and a coarse sand and behind me were rolling hills of moor growth. It was cold to me. I wore everything I had brought and I still was cold.

I was going to do some botanizing and I enjoyed these lichen-padded lands but the plants were in a condition I would expect in New Jersey in the cold of mid-April. Certainly I was early for much of plant life.

John DeMarrais of Pittstown and I had made this crossing from Newfoundland primarily to look for birds, to see what the bird life consisted of in these straits in mid-July and I was hoping to see my first Skua in these northerly waters. This is a species the sight of which has eluded me for some time.

On the map the strait does not look very wide and we figured on a quick ferry crossing. Actually, the ferry starts deep in a bay at Saint Barbe, Newfoundland, and really goes over to Quebec because the landing at Blanc Sablon is at the most easterly end of Quebec but the road from the dock goes into Labrador.

I spoke to a traveler far down in Newfoundland about this crossing and he told me that it took about an hour and a half—if the weather is calm, he said, otherwise it might take up to four hours.

Well, I chuckled a bit to myself about this because the natives always like to pull a stranger's leg, but, believe, me, he was right. Unless you have urgent, very urgent business in Labrador forget the place.

The weather was calm on shore. The little ferry was a big, capable-looking steamer and I looked forward to a pleasant sea voyage. I changed my mind before we were out of the harbor. In fact, at about the time we saw two Parasitic Jaegers harrying an Arctic Tern for the fish it was carrying. The deck was already slippery from spray and people were going down below.

By wedging ourselves between the railings and the engine rooms of the narrow passageways we managed to have fair control of our bodies as we pitched and rolled and twisted along. We saw Fulmar.

The *Audubon Water Bird Guide* says, "Except when nesting, the Fulmar is strictly pelagic, observable only on the high seas beyond the 100-fathom line, which is beyond the range of all gulls except the Kittiwake. It is an abundant species (Darwin considered it the most abundant bird in the world)." *

Some years ago from the Blue Nose which plies between Bar Harbor,

---

* Richard H. Pough, *Audubon Water Bird Guide: Water, Game, and Large Land Birds*. Sponsored by the National Audubon Society. Garden City, New York: Doubleday & Company, Inc., 1951, p. 20.

Maine, and Yarmouth, Nova Scotia, John DeMarrais and I saw two Fulmar in mid-July. We were disbelieved generally and hooted at in some quarters but since then we have been proven correct and this member of the family Procellariidae is now an accepted Summer sighting in the Gulf of Maine and at the mouth of the Bay of Fundy.

In the Cabot Strait between Cape Breton Island and Newfoundland we saw several dozen of the birds and here in the Strait of Belle Isle they were common, too. Since these birds were all in the white phase they were clearly visible as they skimmed along the tremendous waves.

We saw some whales. We were told they were Pilot Whales and I must accept that definition since I have no reason to disbelieve it.

We were managing quite well on what I thought was a stormy crossing. Nobody else was on deck, all passengers were below being very seasick for the most part.

We were well across, I thought, when I spied what looked like land ahead, a large grayness looming. I called John's attention to this but when he turned his glasses on this land he said, "No, by gosh they look like waves." They were.

This is where the Labrador Current took over. We hit it and I thought the ship was coming apart. The sea never looked so large nor a ship so small. It was cold, foggy, clammy cold and the waves were all I ever want from waves. We hung on.

After a bit we came to Labrador. It took two and a half hours. It was an average crossing I was told. We pushed some ice floes about the size of a football field away from the dock and tied up.

A good-sized berg in the harbor had some birds high up on its ice cliffs. Mostly these were black-backed gulls and Puffins but there were some Murres among them. In addition to a few Kittiwakes these were the birds we saw. John got a Manx Shearwater which I missed and there were a few Wilson's Petrels none of which seemed to mind the Labrador Current at all. I think this is all that kept me going, the sight of birds riding the air on the waves as a most normal thing. But that ice bothered me, ice in July, of all things.

And I saw my Skua. Actually I saw two Skua, one going over and one coming back. These were big, brown, heavy birds riding between the waves as if they owned them. John did get a glimpse of the first bird but he missed the second which just gives him a further excuse to make some more sea voyages.

The Skua, sometimes called Great Skua, is a relative of the jaegers. Pough, in the *Audubon Water Bird Guide,* says that this is the world's only bipolar breeding bird. He calls it a robber of sea birds and an aggressive predator. All of this sounds nasty until we realize that life is a system of checks and balances and the Skua is like the Great Horned Owl on land or the wolf in the forest or the lion on the plains.

The Skua captures my imagination. Pough says: "Away from its breeding grounds, the Skua is usually solitary, ranging widely over coastal waters and on the high seas, though in our region it is seldom seen from the shore." *

In the black turbulence of the Labradoran waters, from the deck of a pitching ship against a background of drifting icebergs was the place to see a Skua. I saw him.

The Catskills

Since I have become disposed to viewing a mountain from time to time and since the Catskills are generously adequate, one June day I left Whitehouse at 5 A.M. to visit these mountains.

Without incident and with no loss of time except for breakfast in Monticello I was in the gap west of Slide Mountain at 8:45.

I hold no brief for the terrain between Port Jervis and Liberty. It is high plateau with good air, I deem, but flattish and given over to much traffic and resorts. But as this is left and the upper Rondout-Neversink areas are reached and the hills loom majestically my spirits rise.

And the air clears here, the air gets bright and winey as one gets up to about 2,000 feet and the colors begin to live. The colors on the meadow flowers flash and explode and blaze at this elevation and the air rings with clearness.

It rained in the Catskills the night before and the waters ran off Doubletop and Wildcat. The roadside banks ran water and small streams gushed newly across the road. All along the road the streams roared.

My first objective was over the gap itself to where the road lowered steeply towards the town of Big Indian. Last year here along the road I heard a Mourning Warbler in full song.

At the precise spot of the previous year and within 15 seconds of stopping the car a Mourning Warbler came out to full view and sang its strange, rolling song. There are times when even the most elusive of birds becomes ridiculously simple to find.

* *Ibid.*, p. 262.

VINCENT ABRAITYS

All around me now the juncos were singing. These were the little, simple songs, whirring like the Chipping Sparrows which we sometimes hear in mid-Spring in Hunterdon. But in our county the bird never breeds.

Slide Mountain in the Catskills is listed at 4,204 feet. One has to get clear up into the northern Adirondacks or upper New England to surpass this or down into the southern Appalachians. Therefore, to see birds of a northern flavor the trek to Slide is made.

There is a good trail up Slide starting from the road and this I took. My approach to this business of walking is simple. I do not believe in it. One should walk when no other means of transportation is available. Perforce I do a lot of walking.

Thrushes of all kinds were singing. The Veery and the Wood Thrush, birds with which I am familiar, were easily identified, but I found it difficult to unravel the Hermit and Olive-back, which just gives me another reason for a return trip some time.

The woods were damp and the trail was full of water. It was reasonably cool but the air was humid. Birds sang little although the Winter Wren was heard as were many Black-throated Greens.

The trail was beautiful but, alas, steep. It was a constant grind of up, up, up. After about two miles of this steady climb the Balsam Fir became dominant and the Pin Cherry here was in bloom whereas below it had already seeded. I had walked backwards two weeks in time.

Now the trail broke to the open sky along the western shoulder below the top. Across the valley I could see the tops of lower peaks. White-throated Sparrows were singing.

The trail looped and the climb lessened. I passed through wind-torn firs festooned with lichens. A Red-breasted Nuthatch came to feed in a Balsam along the trail. Two small thrushes, probably Bicknell's, flew up before me. I could see the tower atop Slide.

I crossed the narrow ridge to climb atop a few boulders and could see far over the valleys to the south and west to other magnificent hills and I had that wonderful sense of splendid isolation that comes to one atop mountains. A Duck Hawk passed below and a nesting Myrtle Warbler sang at my shoulder.

I was now high enough to look down upon the top of Panther in the north at 3,760 feet. A slow walk up a gradual climb would have brought me to the very crest. I looked at the sky.

The clouds were piling and they were black. Remembering the weather reports I decided to go back down now. Those Catskill thunder storms are vicious and I had no stomach for being involved in one of the Rip Van Winkle-type bowling games.

I made my way down leisurely and made a relaxed trip homeward. I was back on the flat plains of Whitehouse before six. I had seen a Mourning Warbler sing and had climbed Slide.

Now what can you say other than that mountains are beautiful, that to look down on the tops of other mountains is magnificent, and that the heart vaults where the flower colors leap and explode and blaze?

Vultures, Hawks, and Eagles in a Summer Sky

There is no better time of year to contemplate the sky than a late Summer afternoon. This is the season of majestic quietness, of a resting and a waiting for the wheel of time. Above the ripening aster and goldenrod lies the somnolent whirring of a myriad of insects. Tremendous high pressure areas drift slowly eastward across the continent. Visibility is good. Puffed and frothy slow-moving cumulus clouds, by contrast, intensify the blue of the zenith.

The meek and humble vulture drifts with placid wings upon a tower of air. Before this he flew low and urgently, searching long hours for the food with which to feed his insatiable young. Now the young, too, are on the wing, and he loafs contentedly high in the shadow of the cumulus, supported by an invisible column of heat. Should he wish to visit Connecticut, or his neighbors on the Susquehanna, he merely rises several thousand feet in the thermal, then sets his wings for a miles-long glide to another thermal, and so, swiftly and effortlessly he travels.

On these drowsy afternoons high above the nervous swifts, higher yet than the vulture, a quiet mote upon the clouds, the Southern Bald Eagle makes his way homeward to the Gulf Coast. Ending his sojourn on the cool Labrador headlands, he drifts back to his Winter duties in Florida and Alabama. A migration in reverse, he uses the warm Winter in which to raise his young, and goes north in Summer to rest.

From thousands of wood lots, from the huge valley trees of all the streams and rivers of the northeast, the Broad-winged Hawk rises to test the air currents. He, too, will be leaving shortly, for his journey will be a long one, clear down to the jungles of South America.

In August and September these small hawks will be seen in groups of three or four to several hundred swirling in tight circles in the sky. They have glided to the bottom of some fast-rising shaft of air and are circling upward within it.

Circling within it till it no longer supports them at some high, invisible spot, they arch their wings and glide onward and downward to another air elevator. One may watch them pass all afternoon without seeing a single wing beat. As the day cools and the thermals cease, they drop down to feed, perhaps on some snake still moving at sundown, for they are our greatest control on reptiles.

But the sky belongs to others besides the vulture, the Broad-wing, and the eagle. Out of the northeast to the southwest go bands of swallows, feeding as they move swiftly onward, the Purple Martin, the Rough-winged, Bank, and Tree Swallows all take an early start southward, all migrating by day. Even the Nighthawk is now moving in the mid-afternoon in an early start on the evening's flight leg.

The big buteos, Red-tailed and Red-shouldered, are not as common as the Broad-wings at this period of Summer. Yet on these peaceful afternoons their passage is regular, for not all hawks take the preferred path along the mountain ridges. Even the Sparrow Hawk is a constant transient over our countryside.

It will not be till later in September, near the time when the crows begin to move, that the accipitrine hawks will be overhead in any quantity. It is then the Marsh Hawk will arrive, and we may see such rarities as the Duck Hawk and the Golden Eagle.

However, at this time of year, when the little spiders migrate on silken threads, of all the wanderings in the sky the soothing, gentle passage of the vulture across the tired green of September best reconciles the mind to the fading of Summer.

Plants of the Limestone Land

As we travel northward in New Jersey and the hills become a bit higher and better defined we come into limestone country. The limestone land is in narrow belts between the ridges.

Limestone is a rock that is easily soluble in water and in our state, placed as it is between belts of harder rock, the limestone area is mostly valley. Unless one's eye is conditioned to the various hues of rock the limestone belts are not easily discerned.

Turkey Vulture

THE BACKYARD WILDERNESS

Now and then the whiteness of a boulder or a roadside outcropping will lead to a conclusion of limestone but then certain belts are almost black in color. Across the Kittatinny, between it and the Delaware River, the limestone can be most any color.

Stone types and, therefore, soil types are not of great interest to the traveler except as stone affects topography. But in the world of green-growing things rocks and soils are paramount factors in survival.

Soil types and chemical reactions are not important in the animal world except indirectly. Animals and birds are not confined especially to specific chemical reactions although a few reptiles and lower forms of life are. Conversely, in the world of plants acidity and alkalinity are important factors.

A long list of New Jersey plants will grow only on New Jersey limestone. The Yellow Oak is confined to the limey ridges of Sussex and Warren Counties and Rafinesque's Viburnum. The Prickly Ash is held here pretty much, too. These are large, obvious shrubs but there are many more examples in the smaller types of plants.

One plunges immediately into this business of rock types and soil reactions once the study of ferns is begun. Especially the rarer aspleniums are tied to exact rock requirements.

The soft limestone and the hard gneiss make for a sharp contrast in ridge and valley and this is of interest to the traveler for it is of pleasure to the eye.

Not often discerned, perhaps because as one approaches the loom of Kittatinny becomes all-absorbing, is a belt of Martinsburg shale as a foothill to the Kittatinny.

The Martinsburg bears little resemblance as a formation to our red Brunswick shale. It is noted best as an appealing disarray of rounded hills of molded perfection and of tiny valleys winding around the round-topped mounds.

For scenic beauty the Martinsburg as a geographic formation is best noted between the Great Valley west of Allentown, Pennsylvania, and the Blue Mountain to the northwest. Here it is perhaps a dozen or more miles wide while in New Jersey it is only two or three miles in width.

All of these geological formations can be seen in small review in Hunterdon. In the Clinton area can be found the Kittatinny and Jacksonburg limestone and the Hardyston quartzite.

These formations lie against the gneiss of the Musconetcong and in the Grandin-Jutland area and again between High Bridge and Annandale there is even some Martinsburg as rolling, rounded hills.

It is the rock formation that makes the Pattenburg-Norton country eastward toward Lebanon and south so interesting to the eye and so different from the rest of Hunterdon.

Virginia and Delaware Bay Oysters

A few years ago I was on a trip from a little Virginia town out to some barrier islands, across some 12 miles of bay. On these uninhabited bits of sand were many birds nesting—Roseate, Forster's, and Gull-billed Terns, Wilson's Plover, and Oystercatcher. On the return trip our captain volunteered to show us his oyster beds. And this impressed me, for after twisting and turning over the water in what he said was a channel he pointed to some water which looked like all the waters about and said: "This is my oyster bed."

Since one of those aboard had a bottle and it was a wild, northeast day, this gentleman was sharing it with the captain. I assumed therefore the whiskey was talking. Now I know otherwise.

If you were to look at one of the oyster maps of Delaware Bay you would see it neatly squared off, accurately plotted as to acreage, with the lessee's name thereon. The bay is one huge farm from Prissy Wicks Shoal past Brandywine Shoal to Miah Maull and up northeastward to the limit of the oyster's salinity requirements.

Each man knows his land, or water in this case, and woe to him who trespasses. A stake here and a sapling there is all they need, with perhaps a fast sighting at Brandywine Light, or Fourteen-Foot Light. Or they could use Miah Maull or Cross Ledge or even Ship John Light way up channel.

Up to the last war all the oyster boats used sail, and the masts upon them can still be seen. They have since switched to engines. These are all utilitarian craft stripped of non-essentials.

The designs are unique. Those built along the Maurice River have the sterns cut off neatly in a sharp angle with the water. The New England boats have rounded sterns. Those built along the Chesapeake Bay have pointed sterns with a little platform above. These boats are called bug-eyes. There is one bug-eye tied up at Shell Pile that is reputed to be 120 years old. She is still serviceable although perhaps she carries none of her original timbers and plank.

THE BACKYARD WILDERNESS

At this low point of the oyster business many of the boats have been sold out of the bay. Many owners have turned to chartering to make ends meet, a boat being an expensive article, working or not. When oysters were good over a hundred boats were about. There is nowhere near that number here now.

Of course we went birding, out on the salt marshes, and past the tangled forests of Spanish Oak and Water Oak, thick with gum and with holly enough to please even Paul Holcombe who grows holly at Mount Airy, and over the level roads.

The cold and windy marshes about Fortescue were quite barren. The Boat-tailed Grackles were absent, but the Snow Geese had been driven off the chilly bay and they swarmed on the black muck of the channels, grubbing at the roots of grasses, their beautiful white plumage becoming sadly soiled. Periodically they flew out to the water to bathe.

Rough-legged Hawks hovered over the silent, icy salt lands from Gandy's Beach to West Creek. Short-eared Owls flopped aimlessly above a barren landscape. Solitary crows cut out over the water for the Delaware shore.

But a pair of Bald Eagles had already begun nesting. Their huge nest was placed in a Pitch Pine not a hundred yards from the road. We stopped to look at the nest and a magnificent adult glared down from the platform, the huge yellow beak contrasting sharply with the Snow-Goose whiteness of his head and neck. His disdain was patrician.

On Hansey Creek Road where the wood breaks to the marsh we came upon huge piles of salt hay, some of it still unbaled. Along the road was a string of those curious Old-Worldly hay wagons, the design of which is not seen in northern Jersey.

Horses are still used to draw these wagons; tractors are too prone to sink into the sticky muck. The wagon wheels are rimmed with wide, iron tires that ride high over the tricky turf. This is one industry that has managed to persist although in a limited fashion.

The road to East Point winds lonely beneath the sea-reflected sky. The flat plains of salt-brown run endlessly on either hand.

Beside some dark Red Cedar near the beach rises East Point Light, abandoned, the old red of its brick soft in the salt sunlight, forgotten but to gullwing and cry alone.

Why it was abandoned I do not know. The State of New Jersey is presumed to own it. The ample house of brick beneath the cupola of the light stands empty. The sashes of the windows are gone. The doors are black holes to the interior. The Ospreys and Bald Eagles perch upon its tower and sandpipers run in the dooryard.

VINCENT ABRAITYS

A Trip Into Pine Waters

The rivers of the Pine Barrens run darkly and strong. Their calm appearance is deceptive.

These streams have virtually no drop or fall so that their surface is unruffled and the tremendous water surge below is not detected. There are no falls or rapids or boulders below the surface to denote a flow.

These rivers look as peaceful as ponds and the unwary wanderer is suddenly trapped in a gigantic force that sweeps him off his feet. Beware of wading these streams without first testing the current.

Yet they are good-looking streams, these rivers such as the Oswego, the Wading, the Batsto, the Atsion, and two a little farther south, the Mullica and the Great Egg Harbor. Despite the soggy savannas at their edges they are firm bottomed and easy to walk over.

All these streams are dark, a deep tea color from the tannic acid of tree roots and from the action of certain algae on the iron salts dissolved in them. Only where the water is a few inches deep can the bottom be seen.

Dry sand is a treacherous medium to walk upon or drive over as many a driver in the Pine Barrens has found out. When it is wet it becomes hard packed and ideal for driving.

In an area beyond High Crossing I found this out as I encountered a tremendous flow of water in the road where ordinarily there would have been but a trickle. The wet Summer had brought all the streams up and over their banks. But I had no problem driving through the small flood on the road. The bottom was packed as hard as concrete.

I wasn't so certain of passage, however, when going over the railroad tracks at High Crossing. I scraped the car bottom on the narrow embankment and for one horrifying moment I thought I was hung up on the rails. If I had had a longer car I would not have made it.

If your car breaks down in the Pines you are a long way from a phone or garage and few people drive by. But if you are going to

Oswego River in the Pine Barrens

THE BACKYARD WILDERNESS

worry about such things you shouldn't be there in the first place.

I had these random thoughts as a party of us went over from Maxwell, which is nothing at all, through Washington, which is merely a crossing at the old stage tavern past the place called Jemima Mount, a little knoll of no consequence.

Over these miles we saw no one. If we had gotten hung up on the railroad tracks at High Crossing there would have been no one around, perhaps not even a train to worry about, since only a train or two a day rocks slowly along the lonely rails.

We had come from the Marygold Branch of the Mullica River, where some plants of the intertidal mud had been gathered, and after a visit to Harrisville and Chatsworth swung across the interior of the Wharton Tract to view an obscure member of the great sedge division of plant life.

This interesting and obscure Fimbristylis is not seen very often in the Pines and had not been collected at the one spot for over 30 years. It is uncommon to start with and probably does not come above ground every year. Possibly the heavy rainfall of the year had caused it to flourish.

The Philadelphia folks from the Academy of Natural Sciences had a chance to observe it, as had the group I was with which included Clint Wilson, Ed Laport, and Rey Jones. Very little else was seen in the way of bird and animal life. The Pines in the middle of Summer are hardly teeming with these things.

So we continued on westerly toward Hampton Furnace on the upper Batsto, where there is no furnace. But this is not unusual for lower down the Batsto at Lower Forge there is no forge and Quaker Bridge does have a bridge but there are no Quakers there nor much of anything else.

The bridge over the Batsto at Hampton Furnace used to be a bit tricky but it has been repaired. I always worry about this bridge because to backtrack from it is not easy.

It is always peaceful back in these pinelands. They can be monotonous to some. It takes a long time for a body to note the charm of these lands.

It can be lonesome back in, too, for the places that are on the map have nothing. At least Washington has a sign, but unless you have a good topographic map you would not know that you were at Munion Field or Woodmansie, at Paisley or Penn Place, Long Causeway or Hog Wallow.

It need not matter for all of them are pines and oak, blueberry and cranberry, a high sky and a great quiet.

VINCENT ABRAITYS

A Railroad for Birders and Botanists

The New Jersey Southern Railroad cuts a swath through the Pine Barrens from Atco and Atsion to Whiting. This is the high heartland, a belt of dry sand and low bogs that has produced a record number of botanical firsts for the state.

The New Jersey Southern works southward through the state towards Delaware Bay and it intercepts the West Jersey Railroad at several spots. All along these iron roads are sites for rare plants. There are places like Riddleton, where the Over-cup Oak grows, and near Hampton Furnace there is the Twisted Yellow-eyed Grass, or at High Crossing one can see Pickering's Morning Glory.

It would seem that the railroad builders had the botanists in mind when they planned their roads, so numerous are the plant finds along them. But the botanists, the early ones, being shrewd folk, saw how well the railroads penetrated the remote country and immediately took advantage of this wonderful situation.

From the large metropolitan centers and from the university towns the botanists, zoologists, and ornithologists made regular forays into the country via the railroads. They went all over the state quickly and cheaply. Trains ran frequently and there were stations at virtually every crossroad beside the numerous country towns.

This is why even today the names which are still mentioned in field reports, be it on some insect or some geological formation, are almost always the names of railroad stations—some of which have not been in use for a half-century.

Places like Byram, Kingwood Station, and Ludlow will be in scientific files long after we here in Hunterdon forget that they were place names of our county at one time.

Even today the railroads provide the best means of penetration to both back areas and settled areas. No one bothers you on a railroad right of way, no one appears concerned about you; the engineers and brakemen wave to you.

There are few houses along the railroads, few dogs to yip at the traveler, no cars to dodge or hard pavement to pound. There are no cats to scare off the birds and no roaring trucks to drown out their songs.

The railroads go past the pastures and cornfields. They slice through

THE BACKYARD WILDERNESS

the woods and swamps. They go through rock cuts and over streams. In any country they go through all the various kinds of habitats. They are absolutely ideal for naturalists and all of us still use every railroad we encounter.

The one sad fact is that each year more and more miles of railroads are being abandoned and more and more country is thereby being closed off.

The other day on the usual search for some obscure grass I was down in Gloucester County, in the greensand belt of rich soil where every bit of usable land is in asparagus, tomatoes, eggplant, peach trees, or other crop. It soon became apparent that the only access to the little undisturbed land left here was along the railroad that runs from Salem to Camden via Swedesboro and Woodbury.

This is flat country excepting that the streams cut narrow gorges so that the bridges are relatively high. For some reason in the Cretaceous region of New Jersey, while the whole land is flat the streams are deep with high banks. They have no plains or terraces beside them. On the railroads there is a slight undulation only of the roadbed as the rails run from divide to divide by high bridges.

Near a stream above Swedesboro we found a small wood which still harbored some native plants. Here we found the Chinquapin, a diminutive southern chestnut which has managed to survive the blight. It was in abundant fruit. Here, too, was a southern plant, the Poison Oak. Poison Oak is a rare plant in New Jersey, growing only at a few spots in the southern sands. It is from six inches to about a foot high and should bother no one.

Some curious oaks grew here in a grove. Some of them looked like the Shingle Oak but there was great variation among the leaves and the trees. Scarlet, Black, Willow, Black Jack, Spanish, Post, and White Oak were here, too, so that the possibility of hybrids was high.

Although these were lonely crossings of highway and railroad, the topographic maps showed that we had parked our car at Tomlin and had walked down to the next road, which was Auburn. On consulting Witmer Stone's *Plants of Southern New Jersey* *, which was printed in 1911 making most of the records at least 60 years old, I found that Poison Oak and Chinquapin were both found at Tomlin and that a hybrid oak was called Rudkin's Oak.

Plant collectors long since dead walked the same railroad and they found the same plants we found. Doubtless when my writings have been forgotten some botanically-minded person will run across the

---

* Witmer Stone, *The Plants of Southern New Jersey: Report of the New Jersey State Museum, Part II*. Trenton, New Jersey: New Jersey State Museum, 1911.

bristly burrs of Chinquapin and the oaks that look like crosses at this same spot and wonder what the name of the place is so that he can enter it in his notes.

All over the State of New Jersey are the grades of the railroads. Their names are many: Belvidere-Delaware; West Jersey and Atlantic; Philadelphia and Long Branch; Lehigh and Hudson; New York, Susquehanna, and Western. The short roads—the Lehigh and New England, the Morris County, and the Rockaway Valley—and the various branches to obscure mines and towns and quarries and the big ones like the Delaware, Lackawanna, and Western, their roadbeds are going and their names are being lost.

But those that remain are a delight to travel. No matter the ties were never spaced for walking in comfort, there is no better way of getting at the unknown valleys of Sussex and Warren Counties, the obscure glens of Morris County, or the many secret spots of wilder New Jersey.

In the White Mountains of New Hampshire

In any description of the White Mountains of New Hampshire there is likely to be the story of Ethan Allen Crawford as quoted in *History of the White Mountains.**

Crawford tells how he and his companions in 1823 became lost on Mount Washington during cloudy weather and how they wandered around until they came to the "edge of a great gulf." This awesome ravine today carries the name of Great Gulf and its depths from the heights of Mount Washington are as compelling to the eye as the lofty crag of Mount Washington itself.

The three of us were not on a mountain climbing jaunt but the Presidential Range of the White Mountains cannot be ignored because its alpine character has caused a flora of great singularity and this is what we sought.

We had stopped for a time above the four-mile post to inspect the northwest slopes near the road and here we overlooked the great chasm of Crawford's which he so aptly named. Across the gulf the peaks of

---

* Lucy Crawford, *History of the White Mountains*. Edited and with an introduction by Stearns Morse. Hanover, New Hampshire: Dartmouth Publications, 1966. Originally published in 1846.

THE BACKYARD WILDERNESS

Jefferson and the Adams and Madison stand clearly. The view into the old glacial cirque is beautiful and at the same time terrifying. It is just a little too deep for someone off the piedmont of New Jersey.

The timber line is lost in the White Mountains around 4,000 feet. Plants continue to grow, however, right up to the peak of Mount Washington where an alpine rush is abundant with a species of hairgrass. Even on some of the northwest faces a mat of sedge and grass persists.

The high altitude here on Mount Washington and a few other close peaks has caused a set of conditions approximating that of Greenland and the coast of Labrador. Snow and ice persist late and come early. Snow is in the hollows until June and snow squalls may come at any time. A birder from Pittstown tells me that he was caught in a snowstorm here in the middle of July. Winter conditions come in September. Near all the peak tops are warning signs and they are ominous. The traveler is told of conditions which can occur with great suddenness.

The wind appears always to blow and its force tears at those plants which attempt to grow and prunes them close to the ground. There are fir and spruce forests here only a few inches high, in small hollows between the rocks.

One of the folders issued by the White Mountains National Forest says the needless loss of life in the areas above the timber line has been largely due to the failure of hikers to realize that storms of incredible violence occur during the Summer months. Ice-coated rocks, winds of hurricane force, and temperatures below freezing are constant dangers for even the strongest hikers.

When one sits in the warm sunshine at about 5,500 feet among the yellow blossoms of Mountain Avens gazing across the Summer sky to Mount Katahdin in Maine it is hard to realize the dangers of the altitude.

There are trails everywhere on the mountain peaks and plateaus. In the absence of trees the trails are marked by piles of stones. It seems rather silly to have these cairns only 20 to 50 feet apart in the higher spots except you are told that fog and blinding snow can be the rule up here and that once you are off the trail there is little possibility of getting back on it.

We slowly explored the area called the Alpine Garden. This is a flattish plain below the summit of Mount Washington on the easterly side at around 5,500 feet. This peneplain occurs at Mount Monroe where it is called the Bigelow Lawn and on Mount Jefferson where it is the Monticello Lawn.

The soil has remained fixed on this gentle slope and tends to be protected by a snow cover so that vegetation persists and riots into color during June and July. The plants to be found are mostly the plants of the arctic, hence our interest in these summits.

We started from Nelson's Crag and worked past the head of Huntington Ravine past the Lion's Head to the upper edge of Tuckerman Ravine. Here we could look down into the ravine, a tremendous one, and the hikers on the trails below were tiny indeed. They crawled up the headwalls of Tuckerman's like brightly-colored bugs.

The number of people on the mountain was amazing. They were in all directions. Of course, both the lack of trees and the clear air permit distant visibility, but the numbers were amazing nonetheless.

Trails crisscross everywhere. On our way back we encountered three young men who told us they had just come straight up the mountain by way of Huntington Ravine, climbing up the cliffs part of the way on their own path. It had taken them three hours but their physical condition was so good that when they left us they began running up the steep rock slopes for the last mile. We three crawled laboriously about by contrast.

There is nothing here in the east so contrasting in habitat as the alpine summits of the Presidential Range. Mount Katahdin in Maine as a single peak compares well, as does Mount Marcy and its neighbors in the Adirondacks, but places like Bigelow Lawn and the Alpine Garden are in a category by themselves. It is a stimulating experience to be on these summits.

On another occasion, at seven in the morning, John and I were at the foot of Nancy Pond Trail deep in the Saco River Valley of the White Mountains of New Hampshire. It was going to be a hot and humid day. The trees dripped moisture. The forecast was for thunderstorms in the afternoon.

The trail from the road south of Crawford Notch was westward and upward. At the beginning it looked easy. We began with confidence. In minutes we were dripping perspiration on a trail that was climbing grimly and relentlessly.

We were here for no idle, aimless walk in the mountains as delightful as such a project might be. We hoped to catch a glimpse or two of the rarer birds of these mountains, the Spruce Grouse and a ladder-backed woodpecker formally called the American Three-toed Woodpecker.

Both these birds had been seen on this trail two years ago high up in the great spruce forest above the headwalls which we expected eventually to confront. I had once seen the Spruce Grouse but John had seen neither.

THE BACKYARD WILDERNESS

On paper and in theory this was to be simple. We had only to walk three miles up this trail to Nancy Pond and return. It was not a bad trail, I was told. There was only about 200 feet of headwall to walk up.

Either we would see our birds along the trail or not. At least we would see the habitat. We would see new plants, hear birds on their breeding grounds that we knew only in migration, and we would see a virgin Red Spruce forest. We kept telling ourselves that as we plodded up, up, up.

Being 20 years younger and in far better physical condition than I, my hiking partner made frequent side forays from the trail to look for Philadelphia Vireos among the Solitary Vireos. He sought out the various warblers which were singing along Nancy Brook and in the forest through which we passed. I sweated on the trail and listened to the mountain thrushes singing as we passed through their territories and gasped for breath at every step, it seemed.

We went upward but we saw nothing from the forest trail until we crossed Nancy Brook once again. Then we saw towering above us the walls of the cirque, a panorama of landslides, spruce groves, forest, groves, and barren rock rising sheer from the ravine trail.

And then we were at the foot of Nancy Cascades. These are a series of waterfalls coming down off the plateau. The trail runs beside the falls. The water appears to come straight down and the trail appears to go straight up. Until now I did not know what steep was.

One of the problems in hiking the White Mountains is the difficulty these glacial cirques give to the novice. They provide a rapid entry to the higher altitudes but at their inner terminus is the great scoop which is virtually vertical. The last part of the climb is the worst but then the trail suddenly levels.

Well, I got up there somehow but at the bottom I wouldn't have predicted it. There were Blackpoll Warblers singing all around the Blackburnians and Myrtle Warblers but I scarcely heard them as I lurched up the cliff, hauling up by spruce roots and sapling hemlocks, pulling up on the rocks and ledges and working slowly up by foot after painful foot.

If one turned around there was the great void of the valley to the sweep of the Presidential Range to the east and the Giant Stairs and the awesome beauty of mountains. I couldn't have cared less.

And then we were over the rim and the trail leveled. We were in the ancient, untouched Red Spruce forest, hoary, silent, our footsteps muffled in centuries of sphagnum moss and needles of spruce and fir. A mile of this we traversed and then we were at Nancy Pond.

Nancy Pond is a glacial gouge much as is our Sunfish Pond in New Jersey. It is seven acres in area. The elevation is about 3,100 feet and the air is heady with a forest smell. The higher peaks are close by from here.

All about the pond was the whiteness of blossoming Labrador Tea and the trail ran through acres of purple-flowering Rhodora, the most beautiful of rhododendrons.

We found Rusty Blackbirds around the pond. They came to scold us and John located a Yellow-bellied Flycatcher in song. Winter Wrens vied with Ruby-crowned and Golden-crowned Kinglets in beauty of song.

White-throated Sparrows were around us and scolding Slate-colored Juncos. There were Mourning Warblers in song at the pond and Red-breasted Nuthatches in the Red Spruce.

Did we see our Spruce Grouse and our woodpecker? No, but if we had there would have been no reason to plan a return to this fantastically lovely spot.

On the Delaware River

A trip up the Delaware Valley on the banks of the river looking for the Winter birds upon the water reveals the true sculpture of the stream.

As charming as may be the Delaware in June, a January trip discloses to full advantage the bold, intricate topography so pleasing to the eye. Sharp cliffs and full bluffs, icy rocks and the roil of water are seen fully now and the meandering of the river bed is fully understood without the clothing of vegetation.

Near Scudder's Falls the gulls that sleep near Bristol come to scan for food thrown up by the rapids. Here are the Ring-billed Gull and Herring Gull, and the huge, arrogant Great Black-backed Gull. Between the searches for food they rest on the small islands below the bridge.

Since this section of the river is almost always ice-free it harbors a large number of wintering Mallards and they, too, rest on the islands unconcernedly among the gulls. On this weekend in January there was an Iceland Gull here and his whiteness stood out strangely. The Mallards had an unusual companion also in a full-plumaged male Baldpate duck.

However, the Common Mergansers and the Goldeneye ducks scorn the islands. They prefer to rest on the water or on the cold, wet rocks of mid-river. They tolerate the gulls but they will not mingle with them.

Here at the new Scudder's Falls bridge one is at the edge of the flat coastal plain of New Jersey. Immediately that one goes northward the lumpy trap rock hills of the piedmont are encountered.

These are considerable hills, Jericho Mountain and Bowman's, Belle Mountain and Gilboa, and just below Lambertville there is a fine gorge in the river to make the rapids of Well's Falls.

At the dam at this spot is another good place for the gulls to watch for food tossed up by the rapids. When they are not searching for food the huge rocks make excellent sunning places or they may squat on the dam wall.

Going northward from here the numbers of gulls decreases but a few of them will be encountered up to the Water Gap and beyond. Common Mergansers will be seen, though, in increasing number and where the river is deep and wide as between Stockton and Raven Rock near the mouth of the Lockatong, they will congregate strongly.

Above Raven Rock the blue-jingler argillite cliffs narrow the river bed and where they merge into the red shale at Tumble Falls is the precipitous cliff of the Devil's Tea Table. A series of thin islands provide many hidden channels where the Mallards like to lurk with an occasional Black Duck with them.

At Frenchtown is another stretch of quiet water and this Winter as in other recent Winters the Mute Swans use it as a private lake. The abundant mergansers ignore the swans as they ignore the gulls.

Where the red shale cliffs rise sharply to form the Milford Bluffs appears to be the dividing line for wintering water birds. South of Milford the gulls and ducks are a daily sight. North of Milford they are infrequent throughout the colder months.

Nevertheless, as one breaks out of the piedmont and goes through the highland rocks of gneiss below Riegelsville a cluster of birds is always seen below the mouth of the Musconetcong. Perhaps this small stream washes sufficient food into the river to be attractive to the few gulls and mergansers, Black Duck, and Mallard that are always seen here along with the Kingfisher and sometimes a Great Blue Heron.

A series of limestone and gneiss brings flats and gorges to the river and the river twists and winds over soft rock and between hard to form one of the better scenic areas of the river and still one of the more isolated. The Carpentersville gorge and the Weygadt above Phillipsburg have as much attraction in themselves as does the larger Water Gap plus the advantage of lesser traffic.

While this trip was one to census the Bald Eagles of Hunterdon and

Warren Counties, their complete and utter absence made for the opportunity to study first the water birds of the Delaware and then, when they had dwindled, to admire the fine geology and scenery of the Delaware River in Winter.

For instance, if one crosses into Pennsylvania at Belvidere and goes northward on the newer road along the river a breathtaking novel view is had of the Delaware. If the correct roads are chosen a ride along the Delaware is never monotonous.

The Delaware still has, here and there, on one side or the other, sufficient unimproved roads to afford the traveler a sense of deep privacy and isolation along its banks. The river can best be seen and appreciated from these old, dirt roads or narrow macadams.

The Water Gap was as busy as ever with its speeding traffic but walking up Dunnfield Creek a few hundred yards I lost the noise and among the hemlocks there was only the sound of the creek rushing down over the huge boulders.

A pair of Hairy Woodpeckers scolded and several Blue Jays moved cautiously from treetop to treetop. Black-capped Chickadees moved constantly beneath the hemlocks. Large numbers of cones had been stripped from the trees and lay abundantly on the snow. The chickadees were feeding on these. They were plentiful but no other birds were seen.

The river north of the Water Gap was totally uninteresting in the way of birds. No gulls were seen and but one merganser. The ridge of Kittatinny was cold, uninviting, barren, and with patches of snow.

Whatever Bald Eagles were counted in New Jersey on this weekend were not to be counted here. The warmer Delaware Bay shores and the marshes of Atlantic, Ocean, and Cape May Counties would have to provide the birds.

After all, the Bald Eagle in Winter is a coastal bird feeding on fish and a few Coots and the vast tidal marshes fringing southern Jersey provide a habitat more to a Bald Eagle's liking than the barren frigidity of the Poconos and the Kittatinny.

Springtime in Georgia and Florida

In the great pinelands of our eastern coast the roads run lonesomely onward, it seems, forever endlessly straight to a horizon always distant. Nowhere is this more evident than on the inner coastal plain of

THE BACKYARD WILDERNESS

Georgia, where the stoneless province extends for miles in an undulation of sand hill and clay bottom. This is the red soil country, the famous Georgia red clays are here, like Jersey's Croton soil, berated and unloved, sticky when wet, iron-hard when dry.

One needs to get off the main roads to see this land, away from the garish billboards and the endless line of tourist shops. Take the course from northeast to southwest across the state and see its empty loneliness, beautiful and poor.

Georgia on the verge of Spring is beautiful. The air is a warm blanket and the sun is comforting. The wonderful odor of pitch and tar pervades everywhere. In the swamps, those long swamps of cypress and mistletoe, of Spanish Moss and magnolia, the undershrubs are breaking into bloom and the roadside slopes run riot with strange flowers.

The rivers of Spring are full and thick, the Ogeechee, Ohoopee, Oconee, and Ocmulgee run wide, muddily, and strongly on their mile-wide bottoms. And even the little ones, the Alapaha and Withlacoochee, Ochlockonee, and Willacoochee are bursting strong.

Stay off the bottoms, they tell you, the Cottonmouths are everywhere. I have never seen the Cottonmouth. And stay off those sand ridges, there's rattlers up there. I know the Pigmy Rattlesnake and the Canebrake Rattlesnake should be around and even the dreaded Diamondback. One of the towns along the coastal route has a rattler round-up every March. I have not seen a rattler there, dead or alive.

You will not see birds along the interstates. For birds get off to the smaller roads where the Chinaberry trees dignify the saddest cabins and the Mockingbirds perch on the ridge poles. Along these roads are more Bluebirds than you ever thought possible and the Loggerhead Shrikes are in countless number over the miles; Bluebirds, shrikes, Mockingbirds, Red-headed Woodpeckers interminably on the fence posts and on the telephone wires.

Enchanted as I was with the pine forlornness of Georgia and the azalea prettiness of its small towns, my objective was not sightseeing. I was headed for the Apalachicola River of Florida in the Live Oak and limestone sinkhole country of the northwestern part of the state.

The change from sand and Slash Pine is apparent on the road from Thomasville, Georgia, to Tallahassee, Florida, where around Moncrief's Store, near the state line, the pecan groves begin to lose out to the park-like stands of draped Live Oaks, the strands of Spanish Moss reaching almost to the ground.

I wanted to see two trees in this area, large shrubs really, and I was driving all this distance because this was the only place where they grow, this small section in northwestern Florida.

Both are related to the yew family. Both have counterparts in a limited range on the west coast. Both grow together in Florida and are only known there. The one is the unique Torreya taxifolia, sometimes called Stinking Cedar because of the odor of its leaves. Sargent lists its range as: "On bluffs along the eastern bank of the Apalachicola River, Florida, from River Junction to the neighborhood of Bristol, Liberty County, Florida, and in the southwestern corner of Decatur County, Georgia." * The other tree is the Florida Yew. Sargent lists it on: "River bluffs and ravines on the eastern bank of the Apalachicola River, in Gadsden County, Florida, from Aspalaga to the neighborhood of Bristol." †

This means that the trees are found only on the east bank and in a thin line for only about 25 miles or so. Today, natural stands of the two exist only in scattered ravines. Even when first found they were rare. Today, the place to see the Florida Yew and the Florida Torreya is at Torreya State Park where the ranger is most proud to show them to you.

I got there on a frosty weekday morning. Despite the sign that said camping is allowed, I saw no one in the park. It is in a woefully desolate area for people and most lovely thereby. The MacGregor house, which is now a museum, stands on the high river bluff and one can look down on the Apalachicola at this spot. There are nature trails, too, but the river was so high when I was there that all the trails were under water.

The Florida Torreya is doing well. One may see plantings of it and see it growing wild in the mixed, undisturbed woods. It has long, wide, sharp-pointed needles and is particularly handsome. The Florida Yew looks pretty much like any other yew, attractive but common. However, while the yew was the most abundant of the two when first found it is now the rarer in its natural state. In fact, the park ranger, who said he was a lifelong resident of the area, had misgivings as to its existence in the wild for any length of time in the future. The pine industry which first clears all the native growth in order to make commercial plantings and various diseases appears to be its doom.

---

* Charles Sprague Sargent, *Manual of the Trees of North America*, Second Corrected Edition. New York: Dover Publications, Inc., 1961, Vol. 1, p. 92.
† *Ibid.*, Vol. 1, p. 94.

THE BACKYARD WILDERNESS

A Day for Rocks

In northwestern Jersey there occur several rock formations of Silurian and Devonian time which are represented in the Kittatinny Mountains and the Walkill Ridge beyond it along the upper Delaware River.

As a rule of thumb, if one stands along the southern border of Warren County and then moves northward, the rock formations become successively younger until the hidden, black Marcellus shale is found in the bed of the Delaware below Port Jervis, New York.

However, this is an oversimplification since along the border of Sussex County with Morris and Passaic Counties there exists a series of formations in the highlands whose age is correlated with the younger Appalachian Mountains system of northwest Sussex over the older valley intervening. It was to have a look at these rocks that a friend and I drove northeastward recently.

Our trip began at Hibernia, among the old iron mines in the gneiss formations where the tortuous valleys are recovering as residential-resort areas of New Jersey. Through Telemark and Marcella, past old railroad beds long since stripped of rail and tie, we went towards the base of Copperas Mountain. Here the top of the ridge gleams with the strong purple of Green Pond Conglomerate, a stone of arresting sight, and here the point of contact with the gneiss can be seen at the base of the cliffs. Once over Copperas, beyond Green Pond, the eastern cliffs of Green Pond Mountain glow with the same desert coloration. The Green Pond Conglomerate, a rock of various rounded, colored pebbles set in sandstone, is supposedly of the same age as the less showy Shawangunk Conglomerate which forms Kittatinny ridge.

Northwest of the pond we proceeded on an old woods road till it became impassable. We walked the trail to the top of the ridge past huge blocks of stone among the Scarlet Oaks, locating a small belt of shale which oddly traverses the conglomerate here.

Having had our fill of Green Pond Conglomerate, we then drove up the valley to Newfoundland. Here the Pequannock has cut a decisive gap through the highlands, and thereafter, to the north, Copperas becomes Kanouse Mountain and Green Pond Mountain becomes Bearfort Mountain.

Up the valley between the two ridges where all pretense of farming has gone save for a scattering of apple orchards, we crossed a little of Kanouse Sandstone, but this valley road towards the New York State line is mostly over Bellvale Sandstone and Pequanac Shale. Above West Milford we swung up to the top of Bearfort and to Skunnemunk Conglomerate. All of these beds are Devonian, comparable to the valley area between the Poconos and the Kittatinny above the Water Gap.

Upper Greenwood Lake, which we now circled, had its periodic draining and the scene it presented was like some old conception of the infernal regions. The lake is man-made and in draining the stumps of the old forest are exposed in hideous nakedness, the still sturdy roots in an anguished writhing on the stinking lake bed. But I understand an enterprising native has a flourishing business in delivering these stumps and roots into New York City as "driftwood."

We drove southward on a dirt road, down the completely uninhabited, wild plateau of Bearfort. This area belongs to the City of Newark as its Pequannock Watershed and no hunting, fishing, or trespassing is allowed. So the forest is returning. The White Pine is once more magnificent, and the hemlocks grow stately.

This Silurian-Devonian area was left via Oak Ridge Reservoir toward New Russia where once more the old gneiss is encountered. The gneissic rocks of New Jersey are broken down into three phases—Losee, Pochuck, and Byram—but unless typical outcrops are found it is useless to differentiate them in the field. The term Pre-Cambrian gneiss takes care of them all quite nicely.

An old railbed in the woods and ancient and crumbling foundations among the vigorous trees now gave us the location of the Edison mines. Here Thomas A. Edison at the turn of the century conducted his unsuccessful experiments into iron mining. He innovated shipment of iron concentrates in the form of briquettes, having done his crushing and extracting at the mine heads. These briquettes ran about 65% metallic iron and a by-product was sand from the crushed gangue of gneiss and pegmatitic rock.

Exploration pits and trenches are everywhere. Deep, bottomless, unfenced holes suddenly appear among the tree roots making this a highly dangerous place to go roaming after dark.

At the brink of one of the quarry holes we found the finest set of glacial striations I have ever seen in New Jersey. Ice grooves in the rocks from the last glacial stage are not uncommon atop our northern ridges, but ordinarily they are so eroded as to be hardly decipherable. Perhaps a small vegetative mat here had fortunately protected a fine series of grooves across the bedding planes.

From this area, sometimes called Walkill Mountain, one has an eye-filling geographical study of Sussex County down to Warren County. To the west in the eroded limestone valleys are the Paulins Kill Meadows and the Germany Flats and the Drowned Lands of the Walkill, and then that superb ridge, the Kittatinny, undulates in sharp outline on the western horizon.

Nova Scotia

Nova Scotia in the Summer is a cool and picturesque land, a bright land of color and sea. In the middle of January it loses this dreamland quality.

Under the low sun, under a cold cloud cover it is dour and foreboding. It is a bleak land and the tiny, frame houses huddle unprotected before the elements. The snow remains and the Black Spruce groves shrink in the hollows.

We had gotten over on Chebogue Point, six of us, on the quest for Winter birds and with a few hours to spare we had driven out of Yarmouth to the moor-like farmlands on the outlying headlands. Here was the sea and the surf crashing on the immobile granite.

The sense of coming snow sharpened the air with a bitterness but birds nonetheless were on the ocean, and the loons and grebes dove with abandon into the waters, and the eider ducks, both the Common and the King, bobbed in the inlets with a concern only for us, the watchers.

We crossed a thin-soil pasture putting up a small flock of Horned Larks and flushing a Goshawk from his vigil. He disappeared into the next grove of Black Spruce.

We saw no one on these headlands. On a fish factory pier we had nothing about us except the strong smell of fish long gone.

Under the clouds which had now moved in we experienced a dramatic sense of solitude on these stony beaches. We had nothing about us but the skerry shore and the black Atlantic and its gulls screaming above the eiders.

Even the next morning, although it might be expected on a Sunday, we found no one out on the remoteness of Pinkney Point among the piles of hundreds upon hundreds of lobster traps. We had a visitor here, a small-statured native with a very French name and a talkative disposition.

VINCENT ABRAITYS

He told us that he worked with lobsters for about six months of the year in a highly regulated atmosphere that had tagging and licensing and quotas and little profit. In the other six months he gathered Irish Moss along the beaches. This seaweed figures largely in the local economy for various uses in foods.

While we encountered few people on our trips around Yarmouth we did see a good series of birds. On the road to Pinkney we saw one immature and two adult Bald Eagles who were perched along the road waiting for their breakfast. Here, too, we found two Ravens who were scavenging the roadside marsh.

We did not, however, make this trip for Nova Scotia birds. This was an interlude between the boat trips coming and going.

We made the trip from Bar Harbor, Maine, to Yarmouth on the Blue Nose and we would make the trip back to Portland, Maine, on the Prince of Fundy. Our purpose was to see the ocean birds, the Kittiwakes, the Fulmars, the alcid group of birds and so on who are rarely met with along the coast line.

Our trip back was made in an ominous snowstorm which turned into a raging blizzard out in the Gulf of Maine. Just keeping a footing on an open deck in gale winds is bad enough. Watching for birds in the swirling snow became almost impossible. Furthermore, this boat rolls in a storm. Luckily none of our group became seasick but it was not a voyage to enjoy.

The storm cleared toward nightfall and it was bright and cold at Portland with the thermometer so far below zero I do not want to think of it. But the next day we had some fine birding in the Newburyport area with three Snowy Owls on the ice floes, Barrow's Goldeneye and many Kumliens and Glaucous Gulls.

Yet we had a remarkably fine trip from Bar Harbor to Yarmouth and we accumulated our good bird records on this first leg. In fact, as we waited for the Blue Nose to depart we watched two sleeping Dovekies on the water but a few yards from the boat.

Going down the channel to open water we saw Guillemots and Thick-billed Murres in abundance. I managed to see one Common Murre and there were additional Dovekies. We then had four of the six alcids possible before we left sight of land.

We saw only one Razor-billed Auk. It flew beside the boat far out on our course. We did see two groups of Puffins. These, too, were in flight. Actually, everything we saw was in flight, the wave action making it almost impossible to identify birds on the water.

The Kittiwakes were a treat. These are small, graceful gulls who remain on the open ocean largely, except in the breeding season.

In Yarmouth Harbor we had a fine view of a Black-headed Gull and everywhere we saw white-winged gulls which were mostly the smaller Kumliens, this being recent thinking on their identity.

Red-necked Grebes were especially common. We saw this western grebe both off the New England coast and around the rocky shore of Nova Scotia. We counted upwards of 30.

The trip was marvelous—for birds, that is. While I do not get seasick, I do not appreciate the sea especially in a gale. The alcids can have it.

Some Tough Characters

This has been the Winter of the Pine Siskin. They have been everywhere and I have heard of them from Pattenburg and Flemington, from Oldwick and Lambertville, and many areas between.

Siskins have a peculiar effect on some people. They are tough characters and when they move in other birds had better move out. However, they are impartial and they take on their own kind just as quickly. They dearly love a brawl and they are not particular about whom they brawl with.

All of this has dismayed a number of people. Definitely Pine Siskins are not to be cooed over. Do not forget that these tough Canadians come from the land of the Cree and the Eskimo and you'd better be tough if you are to survive on the frozen, bare wastes of interior Canada and in the spruce forests.

So Pine Siskins have no manners, so they are as cocky as Saturday night! So what? They just don't know how to handle all the prosperity which they find down here in the States. Where in Canada would you find such a plenitude of cracked corn? Where would you find so many trays overflowing with sunflower seeds?

It is just that Pine Siskins are not as blasé as their kissing cousins, the American Goldfinches. If they were to live here in this land of plenty they would soon develop the sophisticated ennui our native birds display at feeders.

So I want to console you by saying that in time the Pine Siskins will move away and they may not come back for years. Then won't you get tired of those cloyingly cute chickadees and those pretty dickey birds, and then won't you wish you had a few siskins around to keep your adrenaline up?

Holgate

There are a number of places on the Jersey coast where one may still take long and solitary walks beside the sea. A few of the barrier islands still have sections where the press of shore traffic in people and beach buggies are unknown in the wilder weather, at least.

The point of land running to the inlet below Stone Harbor is such a place; another is the fine strip of sand which goes north from the built-up section of Brigantine Island. A strip of beach where one may walk runs down from the end of the road on Island Beach to Barnegat Inlet is such a place, too.

Lastly, there is the duned and salt marsh area below Beach Haven which once was called Holgate by all the birders of the eastern coast. Holgate now is under the control of the United States Department of the Interior and the Coast Guard tower is unmanned, and in the Summer in the place where one could park for free the charge is now $2. But essentially it is still Holgate of the vast mud flats on the bay side where the shore birds of half a continent come to rest and feed on their cyclic flow in the year.

For privacy and the least of interference, the season to visit Holgate now is in the cold months, preferably on some gray day with traces of rain and the northeast wind of a disappearing storm. The flat land and the sea and the sky alone accompanies one.

I tried Holgate on such a time recently and with a few huddled fishermen we had the place to ourselves. No one was there to collect a parking fee. It was a miserable day of rain and northeast wind perhaps, but the ocean was crashing loudly in a satisfying turbulence and there were birds about and this was enough.

As always, Holgate was a little different from the last visit I made there, but it is always different as the sea is always changing and shorelines are never quite the same.

The dunes shift and move, make up and disappear, now quickly and in parts slowly so that the change in some places is minute from year to year. But the changing is always there.

Pine Siskins

THE BACKYARD WILDERNESS

The sea breaks over it and runs to the bay. The flats change in position. Long spits of land creep into the waters toward Tuckerton for a few years and then disappear to reform in another decade. Marshes develop in spots that held a dune a few years ago and where a marsh may have been is now a spot for Sea Pink and Seaside Goldenrod. It is unstable land. In the inlet and about it islands arise and as quickly disappear.

Its very instability, the low flats, and low water attract myriads of sea creatures and the algae of rich Barnegat Bay provides the food for the Brant and the clams and mussels and oysters feed the gaudy Oystercatchers who pose impressively beside the fishermen.

We went out on Holgate, slogging for a time through the foot-tiring sands of the beach at the tide line where we disrupted the twinkling-footed Sanderlings. Gulls rose before us, swung over the surf a few rods, and dropped down on the beach behind. I saw one of the black-backed gulls among them so heavily oiled I was perplexed for a moment. It stood hunched and moved slowly. Already the fatal bath of oil was slowing his clock of time. In a day or so the tarred, feathered body will be skeletonized above the high tide line, half buried in the sand.

Busy Oldsquaw Ducks, being always busy, flew in and out of the surf, up and down the beach in a bewildering coming and going. Below the last signs we swung onto the dune area and trudged through the thin grass hoping to flush out the small land birds.

Song Sparrows came up, flew a few feet and dropped back down again. A single Song Sparrow who would fit the description of the subspecific Atlantic Song Sparrow was found traveling with two Ipswich Sparrows. The individual was pale, much paler than our inland birds, a sand-white color about the color of Ipswich Sparrows and half their size.

There were several Vesper Sparrows around and a Vesper Sparrow-like individual, which was a female Lapland Longspur.

A group of Snow Buntings bounced happily over our heads and landed near another dune in search of the windblown seeds on which they thrive. Snow Buntings have a joyful way of drifting along in the air and their happy calls add to the happy passage of the flock.

We had two interesting observations for the day. The first was an American Bittern which flushed ahead of us out of the short salt grass to make its way over the bay to the Tuckerton marshes. American Bitterns are seldom seen even in season, but this was certainly an early date to observe one.

And then down on the white sand a small ghost of a bird would run smartly for a few feet and then stop to become motionless and camouflaged on the bleached sand. This was a Piping Plover and early March is unusual, too, for Piping Plovers to be about.

Dunlins were abundant. They are one of the few sandpiper species which tend to still be called Lead-back Sandpipers and are found in quantity throughout the Winter, oblivious of the cold. These little sandpipers with the downcurved bills are sometimes called Red-backed Sandpipers, depending on the time of year they are seen. The most obvious field mark is the black patch on the breast and stomach of the Summer-plumaged bird.

So with Canada Geese and Purple Sandpipers and a few meadowlarks, plus some Red-winged Blackbirds and Myrtle Warblers hanging around the Bayberry bushes, we ran up an interesting list of birds on the sands and mud of Holgate.

The Challenge of the Everglades and Florida

In a temperate clime Spring is all magic and glamor and color. Even in the southlands the magnificence of the season uplifts the heart.

But the jungle of tropical Florida confuses me. The impenetrability of its hammocks, its forests that are a wall of thorn and clutching brier, insect ridden, its strange vegetation without a familiar plant at all are foreign to the northerner.

The Everglades are not for walking. The sawgrass would cut you to pieces even if the sharp, irregular coral allowed one to walk far enough to keep a pair of shoes on one's feet.

I was thinking along these lines on a recent Florida trip. The inexpressible flatness from Okeechobee south seemed flatter than ever and the increasing abundance of the Casuarina and Cajeput trees, introduced trees which have caught on, were jarring notes. Certainly I felt little affinity to the region this time, appealing as it is in its complexity.

I did remember that less than a decade ago I hired a fishing boat for several hours to be driven over the water waste of Lake Okeechobee until I finally saw an Everglade Kite and this time I sat in my car at Loxahatchee and saw six Everglade Kites without any effort and at no cost. At least the situation for the Kite has improved.

Perhaps my eagerness for the sink country of upper central Florida diminished the awe I once felt for the region running through the top

THE BACKYARD WILDERNESS

of Florida down through the Keys. Perhaps the rolling terrain is one with which I identify the more.

The sink country of Florida is not at all like the limestone country of New Jersey. The sink country is just that, collapsed holes which give a roll to the land. Some are large and some are small.

I was looking for ferns, rock ferns, which meant I must seek the outcroppings. These are virtually impossible to find, at least to the casual traveler. Florida, too, is being fenced in. There are miles and countless miles of fencing of a soundness and height which resist trespassers and are a trial to the naturalist. Apparently the beef business is making money enough to support this very expensive fencing.

The tremendous herds of livestock have ruined the native vegetation over many counties. Botanists 30 years ago were commenting on this. It is a stark reality today.

But I did manage to get to a wood which had the typical boulders of limestone which I needed and had not been grazed. It was pleasant there near a tributary of the Suwannee River—a bit tricky with briers and a bit noisy with palmettos, but pleasant.

Ferns were scarce but the Florida Violet was blooming and several other southern plants. Already I was in the area of true magnolias and a host of other blooming trees with evergreen leaves. I saw the very strange Spruce Pine and I studied the Florida Red Cedar, which is much like ours, and otherwise enjoyed myself.

Yet I remember the most a jaunt I took in Taylor County down toward the Gulf shore. I had to pass through miles of sterile forest which is eliminating the native flora in favor of pulp wood just as the cattle do. I crossed the Fenholloway River branches which were running heavily and blackly but otherwise it was miles of the Florida Slash Pine.

Then suddenly the pines were gone and the soil dampened. The cypress was here and a multitude of evergreen shrubs which I could not identify. A Parula Warbler sang in the Spanish Moss and a Pileated Woodpecker called. The oaks were tall.

The road ended at a cattle barrier over which I drove and the road became wet sand. Evidently I was getting near the coast. This was typical southern coast forest, permanently wet.

For miles I had seen no one, no automobiles and no houses and now there was nothing on the road down which I began to walk—or so I thought.

Out of the forest came a herd of lean and long-horned cattle. I wondered what they found to eat in such a locale, and they could not have found much for they were thin and rangy. The cattle looked at me and they came moving toward me as a group. I cannot tell you of their intent but fear was not in their attitude as I went back to the car.

But it was compelling in my thoughts that here, far from habitation, deep in a Gulf forest, miles deep, were a farmer's cattle. I could not conjecture the miles of fence it must have taken to contain them.

It is near this section that the Ivory-billed Woodpecker was reported some years ago. If the cattle and the paper companies so dominate the scene, how is the woodpecker to compete? I crossed the cattle barrier and drove on back to Perry through the miles of sand with their miles of pine in neat rows and squares.

Cape May Point

Cape May Point, at the southern tip of New Jersey, is as far south as is our nation's capital. It is further south than is Annapolis or Baltimore or the state capital of Delaware at Dover.

Even on days of poorer visibility the coast of Delaware at Lewes can be seen and some 60 miles away is the Virginia line.

So southerly is the Cape May peninsula it is as a region apart from the rest of the state. This remoteness strikes the visitor immediately he enters the town of Marmora on the east or Dennisville on the west, the gateways to the Cape proper.

Cape May is sandy, but it is not the sand of the Pine Barrens but the richer sands of the coastal plain of our southern states. The Pitch Pine and the Yellow Pine are always here but the woods along the road are lush with the leafiness of hickory and oak and gum.

Between the salt marshes of the bay side and the salt marshes of the eastern ocean side is a narrow belt a few miles wide of truly rural southern aspect, farmed and flat, sprinkled with small villages and small clapboard houses beneath great trees along quiet sandy roads.

The charm of Cape May is contained in the sense of high openness, of the nearness of sky and sea, of somnolent, sun-drenched roads and huge southern Red Cedars in the dooryards. But the usual traveler hurries through the center of the peninsula eager for the bay and ocean, disregarding flowered field and shaded wood and bean hullers along the road past old salt-softened houses.

From Ocean City southward to the town of Cape May are some of the finest beaches in the state—white, wide, and inviting. Here and there on the dunes are the remains of the old beach forests where herons and egrets still nest and which harbor a fantastic list of birds in the migratory season.

Whereas on the ocean side the barrier beaches are all several miles from the mainland reached only by the causeways, on the bay side there are areas where no salt marsh exists and the forest and fields run to the beach edge. Tidal channels which allow for an inland waterway do not form here. All the bay marshes fringe, albeit widely, the small streams and ditches draining the peninsula interior.

The bay beaches are all narrow and steep and the dune mainland gives the appearance of a high bluff above the water. This bay side has always been the least developed area of the Cape. While there also has been heavy growth here in the past decade, it is the ocean beaches that have seen the greatest increase in resident and visitor.

The plant life of the Cape has a southern flavor. Down around Town Bank are a few good stands of the Loblolly Pine and the Water Oak and the Laurel Oak of the south can be found here in the groves of Willow and Spanish Oak. Here grows the Pale Hickory and the Black Cottonwood. In a wide and gloomy swamp back of Swainton is found the Basket Oak.

Around the brackish edge of the salt marsh the Rose Mallow was in flamboyant bloom. The Sea Pinks, sturdy members of the gentian family, produce solid flowers of light rose among the Bayberry and Marsh Elder. Water Hemp and Bur-marigold is here in abundance.

Where the Crane Fly Orchis grows back of Erma is found the Strawberry Bush and in Bennett Bog is the Snowy Orchis. Many southern grasses find their northern extreme here together with an imposing list of plants like the Downy Lobelia and the Golden Camphor Aster. One would have to travel far down the Delmarva peninsula to see these plants otherwise.

Since Cape May peninsula is funnel-like, the area acts like a huge trap for migrating birds. From the days of Audubon it has been widely known for this phenomenon and birders from all over the world make pilgrimages here annually.

The Intracoastal Waterway Canal neatly cuts off the extreme southern tip of the county and this is the area where the bulk of the birding is done. Lily Lake and its shore and Lighthouse Pond are always productive.

The expanding magnesite factory at the sunken concrete ship through its fumes has killed off all surrounding vegetation and the Witmer Stone Sanctuary is no more, but any patch of wood or roadside thicket can teem with migrating birds in the early mornings of September and October.

VINCENT ABRAITYS

The Cattle Egret, still a novelty in the bird world, was first reported in New Jersey back in 1952 on New England Road near Higbee's Beach and a group is still here in company with the cows. Terns and gulls patrol the rips offshore where the bay meets the ocean and here at times a jaeger may be found. In Winter there are loons and scoters.

The Garden State Parkway has been responsible for opening up the lower peninsula. The traffic is heavy on weekends and new developments are springing up everywhere. Farming is on the way out; fields are going back to thickets. Yet with the change to suburban the Cape still manages to have a flavor that is unique and those that love the land and the water and the things of it will continue to make this fine journey to New Jersey's southern tip.

·VI·

The Flow of Life

The Great Horned Owl and a Covered Bridge

Between the fogs and whirling snow of January infrequently there comes the fortunate time of the Winter moon. Then the air is dry and sharp and high moonlight gilds the snow.

Deep in the hollow of the night the Great Horned Owl booms the stirrings of Spring and the shining sky resounds. The Great Horned Owl is come to the forest; now he tests his wings. He booms his challenge to the January night and the vole becomes still, the crow sits closer to his bough, and the cottontails freeze in the stubble.

For this is the Great Adjuster of the deep forest and the open field, scourge of the night, fearless and fierce. Yet he is not death but the measurement of life, for his is the task to set the quivering balance between earth and the smaller creatures upon it.

Within the intricate web of life upon the land, immutable and timeless, with its constant sorting, elimination, and rejecting, its constant strife between species and species, its battle between kind and kind, his is the role of arbiter and executioner, adjusting not the proportion of death but the abundance of life.

Unenvied and despised, his is the assignment to castigate and flay the winner and make empty the victory, for in the wild there can be neither triumph nor victory but the constant flow of life undiminished.

He is the reason why no species becomes extinct of its own accord, and why conversely, for example, meadow mice do not overrun the earth. In this ruthless hunting is the protection not of the individual but of the species itself, since in the fine scheme of things there cannot exist too many crows, or weasels, or foxes, or great hordes of rodents.

His sway is undisputed and far. He culls the crows as well as the owls the crows besiege from the Barred and the Barn to the Screech and Sawwhet. He takes the house cat as well as the mice the cat hunted. The young fox and the grouse he takes, the weasel and the rat. He takes the bullfrog the young coon watched and then he takes the young coon. The eagle fears him.

But in the sharp adjustment he also takes his kind for as the earth cannot be drowned in rabbits, it cannot bear too many Great Horned Owls. The rabbits shall not inherit the earth, but neither will the owls.

It is melancholic to contemplate upon the knowledge that those who marvel at the bright feather of a finch and the glad song in May will coldly slay the hawk, not knowing that if the hawk be gone, the finch is doomed.

And in this vein it is in gloom the recent knowledge comes that certain trends in the name of progress may destroy the landmarks of our yards and proceed to upturn the very hearth stones.

Why a simple covered bridge in Sergeantsville in quiet somnolence above a rural stream should so distress certain of our progressive brethren is difficult to comprehend. If the barn sill goes, should the hay be left in the meadow? Cannot an old house have a new roof? Is there no dignity in age or comfort in the familiar?

There is a structure that has satisfied everyone heretofore. It is a covered bridge that satisfied the builders and has carried a stream of trade for decades. It has pleased the children who have grown old. It pleases their children. It has given to the traveler a conception of the serenity of the land and the tranquility of our heritage. It has been the echo of the past in the present. And now they would destroy it.

It is no matter that the Great Horned Owl booms his notes from the pines and hemlocks of the Wickecheoke Gorge, for the generations of Screech Owls in the sycamore bole beside the bridge will be infinite.

Alive and Well

Now and then as we go about this business of living on and with this world and observing it in its many forms and taking it all very lightly an incident will occur that can sober us. We become reminded of the constancy of the world and the inconstancy of an individual upon it.

My chilling incident concerned a grass by the curious botanical name of Bouteloua curtipendula. It is a Grama grass, sometimes called Sideoats Grama from the fact that its small oatlike seeds hang downward on one side of the stem.

It is one of the grasses that forms the grass seas of the prairie regions of our mid-western states and it is a high-quality, nutritious forage

THE BACKYARD WILDERNESS

plant. It is also one of the grasses that is still found, but with great rarity, in our eastern states.

Perhaps it was brought eastward through the medium of great buffalo herds which at one time ranged even to New Jersey. Perhaps the canals or the railroads were accidental carriers of Sideoats Grama. Who knows? Nonetheless, the eastern states are included in its range of growth since it has been found here.

It is known from a series of high, barren limestone ledges deep in the woods of Sussex County and it is known from a single hill in central New York State.

Back around 1875 or so, a century ago in time, it was reported along the Delaware below Phillipsburg by Dr. Thomas Conrad Porter (1822-1901) who, I think, was associated with Lafayette College.

Now not having ever observed this curious prairie grass I ventured to see if it were still growing somewhere along the Delaware River in Warren County, or if its reported presence here was an accidental one of a few years standing.

Scrutiny of area geological and topographical maps disclosed several places where the conditions might be suitable for curtipendula and a Sunday late morning saw me looking down on the curving Delaware from a limestone bluff.

Down the bluff I went where the water had cut its banks into the limestone and here and there in the crevices of dry limestone was Bouteloua curtipendula growing just as Porter said it was a hundred years ago.

Porter is dead and long gone and virtually forgotten but the small grass is thrifty and annually casts its seeds despite the passing of its discoverer and the constancy of the limestone and the Delaware River and the curious grass continues despite the curious eye of the inconstant passer-by.

It appears as small clumps here and there but not over a wide area. One would think that any small catastrophe would wipe it out. Yet despite the railroad, despite the feet of fishermen and river bank wanderers and the high flooding of the river this grass persists in this small bit of limestone and will not be subdued. May it be there another century from now for some still unborn naturalist to find and marvel over.

When Porter was here it was, no doubt, all farmland, but today a large housing development covers the level land above the bluffs. No one can predict what the land will look like in another century at this spot, but I would like to predict that the Sideoats Grama will still be found there, leading its precarious existence in the limestone crevices.

VINCENT ABRAITYS

A Time for Ferns and Lichens

After the frost has moved the greenery of Summer and the leaves have dropped from the trees, the stone exposure of our hills and stream gorges become evident. This is the time of year to begin searching the ledges and cliffs for the rock-loving ferns.

So off on a bright morning to the fine gorges of the Delaware between the streams of the Pohatcong and the Musconetcong. Here the cliff is over the road and the climb is immediate, the river flowing swiftly at the old base of the mountain.

Upon the rocks the mosses grow in profusion. Asking little but coolness, shade, and a bit of rain, the basic rock, offering nothing to other plants, is sufficient to their needs. They will remain green and identifiable throughout the Winter.

As by cautious step and lift and handhold the climb goes higher and the faces of stone become perpendicular, the bulk of the mosses decline and the lichens predominate.

Here is the first step of life; the drying and barren rock, struck fully by sun, lashed by storm, granting nothing but tenuous support, is filmed by the primordial lichen with all the grasp of millenia upon shining quartz and feldspar. The Zoned Lichen is everywhere, like an illusion of rock, its microscopic thickness unevident to the eye, only the concentric rings of coloring proving that this is life, the tiny cell of algae and the thin hypha thread.

More discernible are the gray and brown belts and splotches of colonies of papery lichen and crust lichen and flake lichen running over in struggling competition for the empty spaces of gneiss. On the rock time is nothing, neither the heat of August nor January ice, nor one year nor one century. The lichens are continuous, the first and undoubtedly the last. The generations are so vast in time that man has not yet seen some of them originate.

The hills across the river rise with the climb, and the river threads, the current crawling slowly over the rapids, a delusion of distance. From a ledge with the wind whipping up from below, the treetops under the climber's feet, the valley west of Riegelsville opens to view. Durham Creek slashing through the soft limestone. South of Spring-

Lichens

town, Gallows Hill shows a last glow of October. But there is not enough altitude to see Hexenkopf to the north.

The climb is steep but the trees have been with me all the way. A handful of soil starts them, and the fingering roots search out to grasp at seams and crevices in the rock for support. From frequent wind and frequent sleet the trunks stripped largely of their tops look old before their time, and the steep slope is littered with thin trees, dead in an early failure. Chestnut Oak is here, and Hackberry, maple, hickory. The Virginia Pine is thrifty and an occasional hemlock casts a slender cone of green against the walls of stone.

At the base of the ridge was only the evergreen featheriness of the Marginal Shield-fern, Christmas Fern, and Brownstem Spleenwort. Higher on the rocks in the shaded crevices, safe from wind, came the firm rosettes of the Maidenhair Spleenwort, green and crisp.

The Blunt-lobed Cliff-fern was in its usual plenty, the small sterile frond still freshly evergreen. Higher up where it began to disappear, the Rusty or Mountain Cliff-fern took its place. This is a more northerly plant of high, dry, rocky outcrops and this area is about as far south as it grows. The Rock-polypody is everywhere in thick colonies capping the boulders.

The descent to the road was rapid and I decided to approach the ridge from a spot further up the highway. Here it was considerably steeper, and it was a task to fight for hand- and footholds upon the sheer rock and uncertain soil, but I managed to claw my way up inspecting all the lesser cliffs, and then slowly worked along the ridge below the rim and after a time I found a fine grove of tall rhododendron. Here was Maidenhair Fern in thick clusters, and Southern Beech Fern, and the Interrupted Fern.

Since this was the damp north slope, velvetted and springy with moss, the Fragile Fern grew here and in some of the rock seams were little families of Walking Fern. I was surprised to find a small cluster of Late Coral-root still with petals.

Once again going down was a lot faster then going up and as always a little more exciting, consisting of a series of slides and falls and the sounds of small stones cascading ahead. It was now mid-afternoon.

So I drove around to approach a little known spur of the Pohatcong about two miles northeast. This was an easy climb and a rewarding one. When I got to the bare rock atop the peak, I found the view magnificent.

To the south was the heavy bulk of the Musconetcong running toward Bloomsbury. To the north Scott's Mountain could be seen dwindling down to disappear above Stewartsville. Alpha and Phillipsburg lay on the plain and nearby the smokiness of Easton and the Weygadt of the Delaware north of it.

The Kittatinny and Blue Mountain ran across the northern horizon. There was the huge inverted triangle cut of Delaware Water Gap, and further to the left but as if a stone's throw was the incompleteness of Wind Gap. A Red-tailed Hawk sailed down off Scott's Mountain as I watched.

The rocks here held a heavy growth of Rusty Cliff-fern, and, wonderfully, running along the rock edge was a luxuriant glossiness, Rock Spikemoss. The spikemoss grows only on the highest, most exposed ledges, and it is scarce indeed. It is a delicate evergreen, not a moss, but a close relative of the Ground Pine and other Lycopodiums.

So I left with a sprig of spikemoss in my pocket and the memory of the Wind Gap in the distance and the Red-tail off Scott's Mountain.

A Black Rail at Brigantine Refuge

David Johnson of Center Bridge called up the other evening to say that he had encountered a family of Black Rails at Brigantine National Wildlife Refuge near Atlantic City.

The Brigantine Refuge is a huge, Federal refuge adjacent to the mainland above Absecon and is reached from Route 9 at Oceanville. Birders everywhere know this area simply as Brig.

Near the headquarters of the refuge a series of dikes have been built on the salt marsh to impound large pools of fresh water. The dikes are large enough to carry traffic and it becomes a simple and delightful recreation to study birds from the comfort of a car for some half dozen miles.

Birds swarm here. Feathered life may be observed at any season of the year. The numbers can go into fantastic thousands. Virtually every water and many land species have been recorded at Brig, the rare and accidental ones as well as commoner species.

Those who watch birds also swarm here. Never a day goes by but what some birder drives the dikes to see what is new, to see which species has left or which species has arrived in the endless comings and goings of birds.

It is remarkable that the Black Rail has not then been reported more frequently from Brig. True, it is a rare bird, but the numbers of observers in the course of a season should indicate more observations than has been the case in the past.

All rails are secretive. They live a life among the salt marsh grasses which grow thick and protectingly and the birds are not at all curious about man. They run in the thick grass rather then fly and their call notes are seldom given.

The Black Rail is the smallest of the rails. It is somewhere between an English Sparrow and a Starling in size. It is much more silent than its large cousin, the Clapper, and comes out of the protecting grass less frequently. Doubtless there are many Black Rails breeding along the Jersey coast but certainly few people see them.

Dave saw this Black Rail family in an unguarded moment. He states that the brood with adults came out of the marsh grass to feed in the mud of the channel and to bathe in the channel waters. He had an opportunity to study them at length. He was a lucky birder that day.

I Meet a Pine Snake

A recent incident in the sand country of southern New Jersey re-emphasized anew to me the perfect adaptability of life to circumstances and its ability to persist. This was an encounter with a Pine Snake.

I was back among the Pitch and Yellow Pines of what are called the Pine Barrens in a remoter section of the Wharton Tract looking for a plant which refused to be found.

The inexpressibly flat land is depressing to many people. The seemingly unchanging terrain causes a monotony to those who do not know this country. Actually, the countryside really is not flat. Nor is the vegetation wholly of pines. The sands roll and curve, they dip into damp hollows lush with blueberries, and they climb hillocks where the blueberries give way to huckleberries.

I had come to one of these hillside sites where a few feet of elevation changed the entire plant series. Here were great patches of a pure, white sand formed to crusty hardness. The huckleberries had gone and in their place was a mixed vegetation of open-sun plants. There was Pyxie Moss, Sand Myrtle, and Pine Barren Sandwort just coming into bloom and soft cushions of a Cladonia lichen allied to Reindeer Moss. An occasional Post Oak kept company with the scattered Pitch Pines.

Since my view was unhindered, it was for this reason that I spotted a movement over the open sands, a quick movement which just as quickly ceased. I, of course, froze and scanned the sand ahead. There on a mound of sorts about 50 feet ahead was an enormous Pine Snake. It was immobile.

I walked slowly ahead to within 20 feet and studied the reptile. The head of the snake and a foot or two of its body was coated with a damp sand. The mound on which it rested was perhaps two to three feet across and a few inches high. The snake's coils rested in a mixture of dry and damp sand. Immediately to the fore of the mound was an angled hole which reminded me of a small groundhog hole in some back field.

Obviously the Pine Snake was a gravid female and she was digging a nest for her eggs, the arrival of which appeared imminent judging by the size of her.

She was the biggest Pine Snake I have ever seen, up to five feet long and very thick through the middle. She was handsome, a creamy white with strong daubs of a reddish black across her length.

Since her first quick movement the snake remained frozen, coiled with her head elevated. I circled her carefully and moved to a downwind position about 30 feet away, hoping to observe as she excavated her nest. The snake did not move and I remained until I lost patience.

I moved still further away, surmising that the reptile still saw me. I now was about 60 feet away, so far away that the snake was difficult for me to see. After some moments she protruded her organs of taste and smell which we refer to as a forked tongue. I assumed that at such a distance she no longer saw me but was testing the air for my presence.

Apparently, downwind as I was, she picked up my scent in the area, for slowly and carefully she drew away from the mound and inched to some debris beside an old pine branch where I no longer could see her.

The episode proved several points to me, conjectural though they are. Firstly, the snake saw me before I saw it, which must always be true. Then the snake froze in the hope that I would pass by without noticing it, which is mostly the case with humans and perhaps with most mammals.

The snake knew what it was doing and what its project was. It took no chances with something as important as the next generation.

Even after it could not see me, it could sense me and it still took no chances. It moved away from its nest.

The meeting between snake and me was purely accidental, but I wondered if she would abandon the site. She realized she had been discovered even though I did not come closer than 20 feet of her. Her actions proved her concern.

Whatever her further movements, I am sure they were grounded in milennia of experience, of trial and error until a perfection of action for every situation was achieved and the future of young Pine Snakes was assured.

The Pine Snakes have been here among the Scarlet Oaks and the Yellow Pines, among the huckleberries and the blueberries long before the white man came here. I am sure they will be here a long time.

As for me, I continued on my search about the quiet woodlands mostly hoping that I would not find the plant I was seeking too soon.

Wildcat Tracks in the Snow

Perhaps the cat had denned atop Mohepinoke, high above the Pequest, luxuriously dreaming his sleep in the heights overlooking the valley towns.

But then, too, along the run of Jenny Jump, among the stunted oak and birch, colossal boulders pile to a bobcat's fancy, and certainly in the tumble of the talus slope the labyrinths are dark and dry and enticing.

Certainly in darkness he awakes with a slow and careful wildcat yawn. The luxury of sleep is done. The muscles through his belly are taut, and his nostrils wide in hunger. His whiskers flare.

To attain the summit I had come into the woods off a dirt road near a gap. I proceeded over the irregular, rising ground past old mining pits, up the steep, snow-covered slope to where the great, scoured crest was barren to the north wind.

I broke out of the growth of the close wood suddenly upon the flat backbone of the mountain to face the brightness and emptiness and the circling miles of the valleys to the smokened haze of distant horizons.

VINCENT ABRAITYS

Here was where I saw the wildcat track. The track came down the ridge in slow and measured tread and seemed to pause upon the very topmost ledge.

In the morning, in the eastern sunlight to the northwestward, the Kittatinny cliffs were dark against the snow. The disheveled hills of Northampton were shaded in snow, and the river valley white. Turning, all the individual hills, ridges, knobs, the crest of the highlands, all were capped in snow against the light. The roar of the valleys below in the still morning was muted in snow.

Here on the bald was the thatch of sparse grass and the close-growing blueberries, dwarfed to scarcely clearing the protective crowns of the rocks, and the running of many mosses and the tentacled lichens holding beyond all wind.

Where I in gaudy sunlight saw the ice-mirror of the lake 500 feet below me and perhaps where I viewed the tossing of the hills on the horizon like to Cortez atop his peak in Darien, certainly the cat that had crouched upon this rock in blackness, not seeing the sky of stars, oblivious to the twinkling of the towns, saw the lushness of spruces and tamaracks half a thousand feet below with the intensity of Pizarro, the luckless Spaniard, upon the Land of Cinnamon.

Then with infinite care on felted pads his trail descended to the laurel and down the icy slopes, down to the coned tamarack and black spruce of the morass beyond the lake.

Off the clean and empty peak I went down towards the road, and along the way I flushed a grouse from out of a Mountain Maple.

How the cat returned I do not know, nor just precisely where. Perhaps the cat had found its bed beneath the ledge, twisting deep into a dusty crevice where last year's leaves had blown, and curled luxuriously in the dusty dimness to feast upon his sleep deep in his wildcat ruff.

The grouse would have flown into the maple sometime after sunup. It would have fed earlier in the half-lit dawn on the small acorns of the Bearcat Oak which are still abundant among the crevices. Under the laurel it would have picked the scattered berries of mealy, aromatic wintergreen.

Then it sat on the bough, as a grouse would, in the Winter sunlight to assess the day. With the careful frugality of the wild, reflectively, it plucked a bud. Heretofore they had been small, hard, and bitter. Today the bud had the beginnings of sweetness, it had just the taste of Spring juices.

The grouse reflected deeply, and then plucked another. Beneath the rock the wildcat slept.

Muhlenberg's Turtle

I would like to assemble a small dirge for the smallest of New Jersey turtles. It has fallen on bad days.

It is true that many an animal, a bird, a grass, a flower is in a sad way these days and so little is done, but I lament most for this small turtle because there never were many of them and it carried such a distinguished name.

Gotthilf Heinrich Ernst Muhlenberg was born at Trappe in Montgomery County, Pennsylvania, on November 17, 1753. He was a member of that great family of intellectuals who gave so much to this country in theology, politics, and science.

Around 1770 he was ordained a Lutheran minister in Philadelphia but this city he fled in 1777 before a determined British Army captured him. He escaped and went on to become a giant in American history. Truly, God did help Gotthilf.

Now about the little turtle. It is Muhlenberg's Turtle, named after him, and a prettier turtle in the bogs you will not find. It needs help and if Gotthilf Muhlenberg escaped the British so long ago one can only hope that perhaps the little turtle named after him will escape its destruction.

Muhlenberg's Turtle is small and dark, perhaps averaging three inches in length. When it extends its neck beyond its carapace a vivid orange to red splash of color is seen along its upper neck. Because it is small and because it is colored well it is too often an article of commerce in the pet shop trade.

It is rare in New Jersey. It is uncommon everywhere but in this state a great many herpetologists have never encountered it and the collectors' work upon its population has depleted it further.

I first saw Muhlenberg's Turtle in Tewksbury Township. It was in a little meadow near a stream. There was sphagnum moss there and the Grass Pink Orchis in season. The meadow was too wet for farming so it was only used as pasture, which appeared not to disturb the turtle or several large Black Snakes which roamed the dampness, or the frogs, and they in turn did not disturb the cattle.

But then the usual happened. The farmland was sold and a house was built on the hillside and our new breed of misguided conservationists promptly bulldozed the sphagnous meadow to make a pond since farm ponds are the symbol of the new rich who buy us out.

I do not present a case against ponds. I do object to the pseudo-conservationist and the misguided folk who listen to them and to the chauvinistic ecologists who are giving true students of the environment a bad name.

But be that as it may, there are no Muhlenberg Turtles in Hunterdon County any more. For good ecological and geological reasons, there will never again be Muhlenbergs in Hunterdon because of the habitat destruction.

Some years ago up near Budd's Lake I ran across a hanging bog. It produced some nice plants among the sphagnum and in the alders. I recall the Liparis which bloomed there in June. It also had Muhlenberg's Turtle. The spot had that rare combination of proper spring water, sphagnum moss, and drainage to which the turtle is attracted.

I took Otto Heck to the spot. Otto, like so many herpetologists, had not seen the turtle in the state and I still recall his shout of joy at finding his first Muhlenberg's Turtle.

On that good day we found four of the turtles and doubtless there were others in this small colony. We thought they were in a safe spot. Recently, Otto went back to the spot and he tells me that the hanging bog is gone. The spot we thought would remain isolated for a long time now has row after row of townhouses and the habitat is completely gone. God help the turtle.

If someone asked me for a site of the Muhlenberg's I would not know where to send him. There is supposed to be a spot over in the Great Swamp where they once were. It has been reported in the past from Pine Barren bogs but for so long as I have slogged in them I have not encountered the turtle and I do not know of anyone who has.

I suppose the little turtle was doomed regardless. It was too restricted as to habitat and if one were to come to its rescue how could one explain a concern for a small turtle especially when it elevates a person's status to have a pond or housing is needed? Little turtles with orange blotches along the neck will just have to go. Not even Gotthilf Muhlenberg would be able to do anything about it today.

Shrikes

There does not appear to be a documented instance of a shrike nesting in New Jersey. It has been found in Delaware to the south of us and

Muhlenberg's Turtle

THE BACKYARD WILDERNESS

in New York as close as Orange County but never in this state to date.

The reason for this situation is a geographically odd one as determined by ornithologists. The birds which breed in Delaware and Maryland are in the extremes of the southern coastal plain population. The birds which breed in central New York and into northern New England are northerly extremes of the Mississippi Valley race. They come up the river valley and then by way of the Great Lakes and the Mohawk Valley to breed as far eastward as Maine, Vermont, and New Hampshire. Thus the birds to the north of us are, environmentally, to the south.

Bird students ought to remember that this phenomenon can be extended to other species. For instance, the Red-bellied Woodpecker bred for years in the Ithaca, New York, region before it ever got to Hunterdon and even today the Prothonotary Warbler is more common in central New York than in New Jersey.

Other species which illustrate this peculiarity are the Acadian Flycatcher, the Tufted Titmouse, and the Turkey Vulture.

Other bird students have noticed this peculiarity in shrikes and have tried to correlate this with the presence of thorn or Osage Orange hedges. The shrike is sometimes called the butcher bird since it will impale its dead prey on thorns and the conclusion is that the presence of thorns invites the bird.

I do not think this is correct. The bird does use thorns of hawthorn or any other shrub or tree but it also uses the barbs on barbed-wire fences. Actually, what it needs in sharp points for food storage is available everywhere. Most likely it is a food determination which leads it to specific areas which seem to be open, grassy areas which contain perches low enough for shrike eyes. The bird does not hunt from high perches as do hawks, which apparently have better eyes and are faster than shrikes.

Shrikes do not have talons. They do possess a hooked bill and it is with this bill that they have been known to kill birds as large as Robins but this is an exception just as while they are great mousers now and then an individual bird will be able to take a small rat.

This ability to capture birds and small animals is a well-documented habit but I have never seen it in all my years of shrike watching. It must be that insects are the more easily available food but I do notice that all small birds leave the vicinity when a shrike arrives.

In addition to small birds and mammals the shrikes will take frogs and toads, small snakes and lizards, but the highest percentage of their food is in insect form. They love crickets and grasshoppers.

The bird that I saw on the Ringoes road used one of the snow-fence posts as a perch while it hunted the grasses with an intent gaze. Periodically it would drop off its perch to be lost in the grass momentarily. Returning to its perch, it would swallow its prey.

While I could not see what it captured and ate I assume it was insectivorous since the object was small. It amazed me that life of any sort was moving around in cold light of a December day but the shrike was very busy about its feeding. Its visual acuity must be tremendous.

As are all shrikes, this bird was nervous though fearless. Its agitation appeared not to come from my presence but from some inner drive which the bird had to release from its body. It was all alertness, curiosity, and agitation.

Then, for no apparent reason, it dropped from its perch and in bounding waves it struck across the field and was lost beyond the rise of a hill.

I like to see the shrike but I rarely have the opportunity in New Jersey. I may run across an individual every other year or so if I am lucky and actually try to find one. I have found that if you find a shrike at one spot you may reasonably expect to see a bird in the future at that exact spot. At this location near Ringoes I have seen at least a half dozen birds over many years.

Obviously, these sightings are not the same bird. The conclusion must be reached that shrikes are creatures of habit in their environmental preferences and if a spot looks fine to one shrike it will invite another that passes by.

On the road to Ringoes from Sergeantsville there still are some vestiges of the clean and open fields which characterized the intensive farming a generation ago that was then Hunterdon.

On Christmas Day, a small and nervous bird darted from a fence post along the road and I stopped to look at it. It was a Migrant Shrike. I call it a Migrant Shrike realizing that these days it could just as well be called a Loggerhead Shrike. The taxonomists declare that there is no essential difference between the shrike of the south and the shrike of the north even though they appear separate in our eyes.

It takes a careful eye these days to note that the bird one sees in such a situation is a shrike and not a Mockingbird since the two species look and act virtually alike.

Both the Mocker and the Migrant are a combination of various grays and white and the two show white in the wings and tail as they fly about. Furthermore, they are addicted to perching on exposed points in the landscape, be it a fence wire or post, television aerial or telephone wire.

However, the Mockingbird has a long tail, much, much longer than the Migrant Shrike, and his gray is a deeper gray at all times. The shrikes like the open habitats while the Mockingbirds tend to stay near the houses of man.

The shrike has a swift wing beat. Its short wings beat quickly and powerfully. When it leaves its perch it drops immediately towards the ground and then flies low over the landscape. When it arrives at its intended perch it shoots swiftly upward to it.

The Plants of the Mid-west in the East

A heightening of August color on the land shows that Summer is closing. In the animal world there is still a sultry quiet, but the plants are hurrying toward September.

Along the streams and in the wetter places the giant stems of Joe-pye-weed are especially luxuriant this year as is its near relative, Boneset. The pink of the huge flowering heads of Joe-pye-weed contrast well with the white, flat flowering of Boneset.

These are native plants as are most of the plants found in wet spots, for the wet spots were always here. By contrast, the plants of drier, open habitats such as old fields and roadsides are introduced plants.

When our forests were cut east of the Alleghenies we had no native plants adapted to the dryness and the open sun. The plants of Europe which over the centuries had adapted to man's cultivation of the soil quickly moved in. Certainly they did not displace any native plants. They took over the grounds that our natives could not utilize.

What also is remarkable has been the movement of mid-western plants to our eastern cutover lands. But it is only logical since our mid-west is a treeless land and the plants are adapted to sun and drying winds.

My speculation along these lines was aroused by the sight once more of a plant growing in the abandoned fields near Oak Grove in Franklin Township. I have noticed it in this area for over a decade. This is Sneezeweed, *Helenium nudiflorum*, a particularly handsome plant despite its misleading name. It looks like some kind of a Black-eyed Susan but on closer inspection shows a number of differences.

It is only one of the numerous flowers which through the season explode in a blaze of color on the native prairies of our continental interior. It is also only one of the numerous plants which have come eastward to friendly conditions of growth.

We have another one in Hunterdon County, this in the neighborhood of Prescott Brook and up the valley in the vicinity of Glen Gardner. It is the Cup Plant, Silphium perfoliatum, which is so named since its leaves join at the stem to form a cup. It looks like a sunflower and a very handsome one at that.

In our Penstemons we probably had only one native species, the smaller plant which grows on cliffs and stony hilltops. The handsome Beard-tongue which blooms so well now in our grass fields is a prairie plant. Actually, the Black-eyed Susan is a prairie plant and this familiar plant is a comparative newcomer.

We will never see the Tallgrass Prairies as once they were with the grass as tall as a horse and rider, but we can see many of the components close to home. The grasses of the prairie have come eastward, too.

Even now, along the river flats and on the sandier banks, the Indian Grass, Sorghastrum nutans, is beginning its golden bloom. Along the road near here a whole bank of the Turkey-foot Grass is in flower. This is the Big Bluestem Grass of literature and it grows tall as a man here in New Jersey. The Little Bluestem Grass grows beside it. This is a common grass in this state which we know as Goat's Beard Grass. Switch Grass can be as common in our state as it is in the Mississippi Valley.

Few of the plants of the Shortgrass Prairie get eastward simply because it is too wet for them. The Grama Grass, one of the Buffalo Grasses, still grows in this state however. I am familiar with two spots both on dry limestone rocks where it can be found. It grows on the dry limestone here just as it does in the interior of the continent as we move toward the Rocky Mountains.

It would be interesting sometime just to list all those plants which grow in the east whose ancestral home is west of the mountains. It would be a surprisingly long list.

Bird Watching in the Shadow of an Airport

A trip to Tinicum Wildlife Refuge near Philadelphia is one of incongruities. Yet the area is and has always been one of the finest waterfowl stopping places on the eastern coast.

THE BACKYARD WILDERNESS

One must make his way through the desolation of South Philadelphia to attain the refuge, past the refineries stretching continuously along the Schuylkill and through the traffic of the municipal airport. In the weedy wilderness west of the airport the way is through a long abandoned development with only an occasionally occupied house.

Fortunately there are signs for the refuge else one would quickly lose his way among the untended, rutted streets piled high with rubbish and debris. Finally the dikes are come upon and the road is between the waterways and the wet marshland.

The spot, which is now part of the Philadelphia park system, is merely a low bog along Darby Creek which affords many pools and soggy marshes for rails and ducks. Properly, all this peninsula, which now includes the Philadelphia International Airport, from the Schuylkill River to Essington and between Darby Creek and the Delaware River can be called Tinicum and at one time all of it was a famous birding section for Philadelphians and their neighbors.

Today, the refuge is squeezed along the east bank of Darby Creek. There is a further prospect that it will be narrowed and confined by Interstate 95 which is being built along its eastern edges. It is doubtful that it will be completely eliminated however.

Tinicum is noted first for its duck population. Its proximity to the Delaware River and Bay and their vast tidal reaches gives the birds a superlative feeding ground. Darby Creek and the Schuylkill River provide fresh water for those fowl who demand it.

This is a famous wintering ground for the Pintail Duck with populations up to 15,000 being noted. The Pintails remain here so exclusively that they are a rare duck a few miles eastward along the Atlantic coast. The Tinicum population makes the Pintails the most abundant migratory duck in the Delaware River Valley in Spring and Fall.

Many other species linger at Tinicum. It is an excellent spot for such rarities as the Golden Plover and the Buff-breasted Sandpiper. It is as good as the Atlantic coast for the prospects of seeing a Ruff or Reeve or a European Teal.

A trip to the refuge ought to include the side journey to the eastern edges of Philadelphia International Airport. Here, at the end of the runways, one may have the huge jets scream unmercifully overhead and the thick exhausts settle around one as the Horned Larks and Pipits are studied. The short-cropped grass attracts such birds as the Black-bellied Plover and many others.

The birds pay no more attention to the steady stream of planes departing overhead than do the Pintails a few miles to the west to the continual approaches of the same planes. The whole trip to the area is a complete anomaly to usual birding.

Crows

Gone now are the days of aster and gold when the bees droned the dwindling Summer. The dewed mornings are bell clear.

A tremendous surge of geese has gone down the land. Long lines of them, great wedges thrust their way southward and the cries of them were old remembrances.

We have a new set of crows. Ours are gone and daily small groups come from the north and caw their way southward. There are always some who stay to feed a time and then go on to be replaced by others, perhaps from farther north.

The Winter crows give a pleasant sound to the landscape and there is more than enough corn to feed them without incurring any farmer's wrath. In fact, it has been many years since I have heard any criticism of crows by our farmers.

Provided there is no necessity to outwit them, which man cannot do, crows are nice birds to have around. They are curious, good natured, and always ready for a little excitement—such as mobbing a hawk or an owl.

Man and his works fascinate the crows and they are ready to visit at any time, cautiously, and the sound of their caucus is an appeaing part of a Winter's day.

When the Brown Turns to Green

When in the late Winter woods the eye is assailed by a preponderance of browns and blacks. The color of the country is in keeping with a dreary season, gray stone and dark wood and brown leaves everywhere.

A squirrel is seen at great distance then and a grouse may be seen at a greater distance than the rumble of its wings may be heard.

A land in Winter has little secret. A bird's flight may be reckoned through an entire wood.

Crow

THE BACKYARD WILDERNESS

But now a faint wind of green is on the trees. We tally Spring by green. Yet at first the Spring was all liquid.

Spring was drops and trickles of water, rills and rivulets numbing cold and glassy clear. Water was in pools and ditches, sodden leaves and slippery ice. It was foaming streams and booming brooks and the liquid running everywhere. Spring was the river rising from the mountain snow.

Water was a solvent and a solidifier, a cleanser and an intricate medium, a catalyst of the seasons in the change from brown to green.

In that period of time it was only the salamanders breeding by wet and shivering courtship. Spring was Hyla crucifer, the Peeper who piped upon the soggy meadows and the drowned land.

And afterwards only was the Spring a green, a chlorophyll of sun. But there was another interim. This was the space of the wild geese flying. It was the time of sound when the high, speeding Canadas honked to a sterile world and all eyes turned to the northward struggling line of fowl.

And as the eyes lifted to the crying line fighting northward the Winter-deadened hearts lifted to Spring.

And also before any green the Wood Duck came. The trees stood darkly in the wooded pools and among them his color glowed. He was like a flower of many colors. He was like a fire.

He came with a mate to the wooded swamps of March so his whispered quacking was already a private sound. All the greens, reds, and whites, the chestnuts and grays were an explosion of color of a secret kind, of a private nature. But it was before the Spring if we count Spring by green of lawn and green of wood.

On Wawayanda Mountain and Kittatinny before even a suggestion of green the Wood Frogs clatter in rattling din in all the mountain bogs. The thick fog in the gorges starts a wildcat yowl. The Wood Rats carry sticks all night long.

So many things may serve for Spring. Geese flight and fox bark, these may serve, but alder catkins and Cricket Frogs may do as well.

Spring is a compound. It is a measurable thing composed of undelineated intangibles. For instance, it is a March wind howling insanely and without purpose—or, purposely, it is a reasonable March gale to evaporate the unreasonable amounts of Winter water.

But Spring is best in an April dawn when the young tufts of grass are just tall enough to hold their single drop of dew, when phoebes sing and the air is still. In an April morning we will concede to green.

It does not matter whether this or that is really Spring, the peculiar sound or the particular time, eventually we accede to green.

Sunlight and April zephyrs, maple buds, and Robin song are all within the scope of the magic greens, the green of meadow grass, the green of wooded hill.

This is the green that the rabbit nibbles, that the deer crunch, that the Painted Turtle sees from his water-soaked log.

It is the green of all purposes. It hides the vireo's nest and feeds the worms the Redstart garners. It makes young woodchucks fat for the vixen's young.

In a few short weeks we shall live in an ocean of green. In quick time so much of green will be around us that the mind will accept it as permanency not remembering the Winter when the wood was open and the world was dull brown and stone gray.

But now Spring is a wonder and a miracle and a great, singing joy of green.

Bibliography

The best reference for field identification and study remains *A Field Guide to the Birds* by Roger Tory Peterson (Boston: Houghton Mifflin Co., 1947).

Others in the Peterson Field Guide Series, edited by Mr. Peterson and published by Houghton Mifflin Co., which are especially recommended are:

A Field Guide to Western Birds by Roger Tory Peterson;

A Field Guide to the Butterflies (Eastern North America) by Alexander B. Klots;

A Field Guide to Reptiles and Amphibians (Eastern North America) by Roger Conant;

A Field Guide to Rocks and Minerals by Frederick H. Pough; and

A Field Guide to Wildflowers (Northeastern and North-central North America) by Roger Tory Peterson and Margaret McKenny.

A good reference library could include general and regional works such as the following:

Brockman, C. Frank. *Trees of North America: A Field Guide to the Major Native and Introduced Species North of Mexico.* New York: Golden Press, Western Publishing Co., Inc., 1966.

Bull, John. *Birds of the New York Area.* New York: Harper and Row, Publishers, 1964.

Burt, William H. and Richard P. Grossenheider. *A Field Guide to the Mammals.* Boston: Houghton Mifflin Co., 1952.

Chrysler, M. A. and J. L. Edwards. *The Ferns of New Jersey including the Fern Allies.* New Brunswick, N.J.: Rutgers University Press, 1947.

Fables, David, Jr. *Annotated List of New Jersey Birds.* Newark, N.J.: Urner Ornithological Club of the Newark Museum, 1955.

Gleason, Henry A. and Arthur Cronquist. *Manual of Vascular Plants of Northeastern United States and Adjacent Canada.* Princeton, N.J.: D. Van Nostrand Co., Inc., 1963.

Kauffeld, Carl. *Snakes and Snake Hunting.* Garden City, N.Y.: Hanover House, 1957.

BIBLIOGRAPHY

Nearing, G. G. *The Lichen Book.* Ridgewood, N.J.: Published by the Author, 1947.

Peterson, Roger Tory. *How to Know the Birds: An Introduction to Bird Recognition.* Boston: Houghton Mifflin Co., 1949.

Pettingill, Olin Sewall, Jr. *A Guide to Bird Finding East of the Mississippi.* New York: Oxford University Press, 1951.

——— *A Guide to Bird Finding West of the Mississippi.* New York: Oxford University Press, 1953.

Pough, Richard H. *Audubon Bird Guide: Small Land Birds of Eastern and Central North America.* Garden City, N.Y.: Doubleday and Co., 1946.

——— *Audubon Water Bird Guide: Water, Game and Large Land Birds of Eastern and Central North America from Southern Texas to Central Greenland.* Garden City, N.Y.: Doubleday and Co., 1951.

Radford, Albert E., Harry E. Ahles, and C. Ritchie Bell. *Manual of the Vascular Flora of the Carolinas.* Chapel Hill, N.C.: University of North Carolina Press, 1964, 1968.

Robbins, Chandler S., Bertel Bruun, and Herbert S. Zim. *Birds of North America: A Guide to Field Identification.* New York: Golden Press, Western Publishing Co., Inc., 1966.

Wherry, Edgar T. *The Fern Guide: Northeastern and Midland United States and Adjacent Canada.* Garden City, N.Y.: Doubleday and Co., 1961.

Journals, periodicals, and magazines are issued by many organizations devoted to plants and birds. These are always informative and sometimes more so than books since their material is always current and local. Listed below is a limited sampling.

American Birds—Incorporating Audubon Field Notes, published by the National Audubon Society, 950 Third Avenue, New York, New York 10022.

Audubon—The Magazine of the National Audubon Society, 950 Third Avenue, New York, New York 10022.

The Auk—A Quarterly Journal of Ornithology, published by the American Ornithologists' Union, National Museum of Natural History, Smithsonian Institution, Washington, D.C. 20560.

Bartonia—Journal of the Philadelphia Botanical Club, published by the Club, Academy of Natural Sciences, 19th & Parkway, Philadelphia, Pennsylvania 19103.

BIBLIOGRAPHY

Birding, published by the American Birding Association, Inc., Box 4335, Austin, Texas 78765.

Bulletin of the Torrey Botanical Club, published by the Club, New York Botanical Garden, Bronx, New York 10458.

Cassinia, published by the Delaware Valley Ornithological Club, Academy of Natural Sciences, 19th & Parkway, Philadelphia, Pennsylvania 19103.

Castanea—The Journal of the Southern Appalachian Botanical Club, published for the Club at West Virginia University, Morgantown, West Virginia.

New Jersey Nature News, published by New Jersey Audubon Society, 790 Ewing Avenue, Franklin Lakes, New Jersey 07417.

Rhodora—Journal of the New England Botanical Club, published by the Club, Botanical Museum, Oxford Street, Cambridge, Massachusetts 02138.

Urner Field Observer, published by the Urner Ornithological Club, Newark Museum, Newark, New Jersey.

The Wilson Bulletin, published by the Wilson Ornithological Society, c/o Museum of Zoology, University of Michigan, Ann Arbor, Michigan 48104.

Index

Agaric
  Fly (*Amanita muscaria*), 101
  Royal (*Amanita caesarea*), 101
Agaricus, 102
Alexanders, see Golden Alexanders
Alyssum, Hoary (*Alyssum alyssoides*), 108, 109
American Lotus (*Nelumbo lutea*), 86
Anise Root (*Osmorhiza longistylis*), 28
Arethusa (*Arethusa bulbosa*), 88-92
Arrow-wood (*Viburnum recognitum*), 29
Ash
  Black (*Fraxinus nigra*), 41
  Green (*Fraxinus pennsylvanica*), 41
  Mountain (*Pyrus americana*), 34, 127
  Prickly (*Xanthoxyllum americanum*), 137
  Red (*Fraxinus tomentosa*), 41
  White (*Fraxinus americanus*), 41
Aster, Golden Camphor (*Heterotheca subaxillaris*), 167
Auk
  Great (*Pinguinus impennis*), 126
  Razor-billed (*Alca torda*), 158
Avens, Mountain (*Geum Peckii*), 147
Awned Meadow Beauty (*Rhexia aristosa*), 79, 80

Baldpate (*Mareca americana*), 150
Barberry, Japanese (*Berberis Thunbergii*), 26
Bartram's Sandpiper, see Plover, Upland
Basil (*Ocimum Basilicum*), 108
Bat
  Big Brown (*Eptesicus fuscus*), 110
  Hoary (*Lasiurus cinereus*), 110, 113
  Red (*Lasiurus borealis*), 110
  Silver-haired (*Lasionycteris noctivagans*), 110, 113
Bayberry (*Myrica pensylvanica*), 35, 38, 164, 167
Beach Heather, see Hudsonia
Bearberry (*Arctostaphylos uva-ursi*), 92
Beard-tongue (*Penstemon Digitalis*), 190
Bear Grass (*Xerophyllum tenax*), 92

Bittern, American (*Botaurus lentiginosus*), 67, 163
Blackbird
  Brewer's (*Euphagus cyanocephalus*), 105
  Red-winged (*Agelaius phoeniceus*), 105, 164
  Rusty (*Euphagus carolinus*), 105, 150
  Yellow-headed (*Xanthocephalus xanthocephalus*), 105
Black-eyed Susan (*Rudbeckia serotina*), 27, 37, 189, 190
Black Haw (*Viburnum prunifolium*), 38, 46, 125
Blazing Star (*Liatris spicata*), 38, 39, 40
Bluebird, Eastern (*Sialia sialis*), 153
Blushing Venenarius (*Amanita rubescens*), 101
Bobolink (*Dolichonyx oryzivorous*), 26, 33, 105
Boneset (*Eupatorium perfoliatum*), 189
Bouncing Bet (*Saponaria officinalis*), 35
Bouteloua curtipendula, see Grama, Side-oats
Brant (*Branta bernicla*), 53, 163
Broom Crowberry (*Corema Conradii*), 92
Brown Thrasher (*Toxostoma rufum*), 47
Bunting
  Indigo (*Passerina cyanea*), 27, 33, 34, 70
  Snow (*Plectrophenax nivalis*), 40, 163
Bur Marigold (*Bidens laevis*), 167
Burnet (*Sanguisorba canadensis*), 24
Buttercup, Bulbous (*Ranunculus bulbosus*), 29
Butterfly, Monarch (*Danaus plexippus*), 118-120

Cajeput (*Melaleuca quinquenervia*), 164
Candelita, see Redstart, American
Caper Plant, see Mole Spurge

— 200 —

INDEX

Cardinal (*Richmondena cardinalis*), *xiii*, *xvii*, 26, 47, 61
Carex
  stricta, 24
  Tuckerman's (*Carex Tuckermani*), *xviii*
Casuarina (*Casuarina equisetifolia*), 164
Catbird (*Dumetella carolinensis*), 26, 29
Cedar
  Florida Red (*Juniperus silicicola*), 165
  Red (*Juniperus virginiana*), 38, 108, 139, 166
  Stinking, see Torreya, Florida
Chamomile (*Anthemis nobilis*), 108
Chara, 93
Chat, Yellow-breasted (*Icteria virens*), 25, 35
Cherry
  Choke (*Prunus virginiana*), 97
  Fire (*Prunus pensylvanica*), 98, 132
  Oxheart (*Prunus Avium*), 97, 98
  Pin, see Fire Cherry
  Rum (*Prunus serotina*), 97
  Sand (*Prunus depressa*), 98
  Sour (*Prunus Cerasus*), 97
  Sweet, see Oxheart Cherry
Chestnut, Dwarf, see Chinquapin
Chickadee, Black-capped (*Parus atricapillus*), 152
Chicory (*Cichorium Intybus*), 35, 37
Chinaberry (*Melia Azederach*), 153
Chinquapin (*Castanea pumila*), 85, 86, 145, 146
Cicada Killer (*Sphecius speciosus*), 121
Cicely (*Myrrhis odorata*), 108
Cladonia lichen, 180
Coot, American (*Fulica americana*), 152
Copperhead (*Agkistrodon contortix*), 115, 116
Coreopsis rosea, see Tickseed
Coral-root, Late (*Corallorhiza odontorhiza*), 177
Cottonmouth, Eastern (*Agkistrodon p. piscivorus*), 115, 153
Cowbird, Brown-headed (*Molothrus ater*), 105
Crow, Fish (*Corvus ossifragus*), 79
Cuckoo-flower (*Cardamine pratensis*), 93
Cup Plant (*Silphium perfoliatum*), 190
Cypress, Bald (*Taxodium distichum*), 99, 100

Daisy, Ox-eye (*Chrysanthemum Leucanthemum*), 23
Dandelion, Common (*Taraxacum officinale*), 27
Destroying Angel (*Amanita phalloides*), 101
Diamondback, Eastern (*Crotalus adamenteus*), 153
Dogwood, Flowering (*Cornus florida*), 28, 38, 106
Dovekie (*Plautus alle*), 125, 158
Dragon's Mouth, see Arethusa
Duck
  Barrow's Goldeneye (*Bucephala islandica*), 158
  Black (*Anas rubripes*), 151
  Canvasback (*Aythya valisneria*), 77
  Common Goldeneye (*Bucephala clangula*), 77, 150
  Harlequin (*Histrionicus histrionicus*), 78
  Labrador (*Camptorhynchus labradoricus*), 126
  Mallard (*Anas platyrhynchos*), 150, 151
  Oldsquaw (*Clangula hyemalis*), 163
  Pintail (*Anas acuta*), 191
  Wood (*Aix sponsa*), 195
Dunlin (*Erolia alpina*), 84, 164

Eagle
  Golden (*Aquila chrysaetos*), 65, 134
  Southern Bald (*Haliaetus leucocephalus*), *xiii*, 65, 67, 133, 139, 151, 152, 158
Egret
  Cattle (*Bubulcus ibis*), 67, 168
  Snowy (*Leucophoyx thula*), 79
Eider
  Common (*Somateria molissima*), 78, 157
  King (*Somateria spectabilis*), 78, 157

Falcon, Peregrine (*Falco peregrinus*), *xiii*, *xiv*, 65, 67, 132, 134
Featherfoil (*Hottonia inflata*), 93
Fern
  Blunt-lobed Cliff (*Woodsia obtusa*), 177
  Christmas (*Polystichum acrostichoides*), 177
  Cinnamon (*Osmunda cinnamomea*), 24
  Curly Grass (*Schizaeapusilla*), 91
  Fragile (*Cystopteris fragilis*), 177

INDEX

Interrupted (*Osmunda Claytoniana*), 177
Maidenhair (*Adiantum pedatum*), 177
Marginal Shield (*Dryopteris marginalis*), 177
Marsh (*Dryopteris thelypteris*), 23, 24, 25
Mountain Cliff, see Rusty Cliff
Rusty Cliff (*Woodsia ilvensis*), 177, 178
Southern Beech (*Dryopteris hexagonoptera*), 177
Walking (*Camptosorus rhizophyllus*), 177
Fetterbush (*Leucothoe racemosa*), 91
Fiddler Crab (*Gelasimus* genus), 87
Finch
 House (*Carpodacus mexicanus*), 47, 48
 Purple (*Carpodacus purpureus*), 47, 48, 61
Fir, Balsam (*Abies balsamea*), 132
Fleabane, Salt Marsh (*Pluchea purpurascens*), 79
Flicker, Yellow-shafted (*Colaptes auratus*), 23, 53
Floating-heart, European Yellow (*Nymphoides peltata*), 85
Fly
 Harvest (*Cicadidae* family), 88
 House (*Musca domestica*), 106
Flycatcher
 Acadian (*Empidonax virescens*), 187
 Alder (Traill's) (*Empidonax traillii*), 23
 Ash-throated (*Myiarchus cinerascens*), 48
 Least (*Empidonax minimus*), 35
 Yellow-bellied (*Empidonax flaviventris*), 150
Fly Poison, see Agaric, Fly
Fox
 Arctic (*Alopex lagopus*), 84
 Red (*Vulpes fulva*), 48
Frog
 Cricket (*Acris crepitans*), 25, 195
 Green (*Rana clamitans*), 25
 Wood (*Rana sylvatica*), 195
Fulmar (*Fulmarus glacialis*), 129, 130, 158

Gannet (*Morus bassanus*), 78
Garlic
 Field (*Allium vineale*), 94
 Wild (*Allium canadense*), 94
Gentian, Fringed (*Gentiana crinita*), 45
Germander (*Teucrium Chamaedrys*), 108
Golden Alexanders (*Zizia aurea*), 27, 28
Golden Ragwort (*Senecio aureus*), 28
Goldenrod, Seaside (*Solidago sempervirens*), xix, 118, 163
Goldfinch, American (*Spinus tristis*), 47, 159
Goose
 Canada (*Branta canadensis*), 164, 195
 Snow (*Chen hyperborea*), 53, 139
Goshawk (*Accipiter gentilis*), 65, 157
Grackle
 Boat-tailed (*Cassidix mexicanus*), 105, 139
 Purple (*Quiscalus quiscula*), 105
Grama, Sideoats (*Bouteloua curtipendula*), 172-173, 190
Grass
 Allegheny Fly-back, see Poverty Grass
 Beard (*Andropogon scoparius*), 38, 190
 Big Bluestem (*Andropogon Gerardi*), 190
 Buffalo, see Grama Grass
 Goat's Beard, see Beard Grass
 Grama, see Grama, Sideoats
 Indian (*Sorghastrum nutans*), 38, 190
 Little Bluestem, see Beard Grass
 Moon-shine, see Poverty Grass
 Parnassus (*Parnassia glauca*), 45
 Poverty (*Danthonia compressa*), 127
 Sweet Vernal (*Anthoxanthum odoratum*), 28
 Switch (*Panicum virgatum*), 190
 Turkey-foot, see Big Bluestem Grass
 Twisted Yellow-eye (*Xyris flexuosa*), 144
Grebe
 Horned (*Podiceps auritus*), 77
 Red-necked (*Podiceps grisegena*), 159
Grosbeak
 Evening (*Hesperiphona vespertina*), 48, 61
 Rose-breasted (*Pheucticus ludovicianus*), 26, 35
Ground Pine (*Lycopodium flabelliforme*), 178
Groundsel, see Golden Ragwort

INDEX

Grouse, Spruce (*Canachites canadensis*), 148, 150
Guillemot, Black (*Cepphus grylle*), 158
Gull
  Black-headed (*Larus ridibundas*), 159
  Glaucous (*Larus hyperborea*), 158
  Great Black-backed (*Larus marinus*), 150
  Herring (*Larus argentatus*), 150
  Iceland (*Larus glaucodea*), 150, 158, 159
  Kumlien's, see Iceland Gull
  Laughing (*Larus atricilla*), 87
  Ring-billed (*Larus delawarensis*), 150
Gum
  Sour (*Nyssa sylvatica*), 23, 25, 59, 78, 99, 100
  Sweet (*Liquidambar styraciflua*), 78, 84, 100
Gyrfalcon (*Falco rusticolus*), 84, 126

Hackberry (*Celtis occidentalis*), 42, 45, 177
Hawk
  Broad-winged (*Buteo platypterus*), 65, 107, 115, 133, 134
  Duck, see Falcon, Peregrine
  Marsh (*Circus cyaneus*), 65, 134
  Red-shouldered (*Buteo lineatus*), xiii, 65, 107, 134
  Red-tailed (*Buteo jamaicensis*), 23, 65, 67, 107, 134, 178
  Rough-legged (*Buteo lagopus*), 139
  Sharp-shinned (*Accipiter striatus*), 65
  Sparrow (*Falco sparverius*), 65, 134
Hawthorn, English (*Crataegus mongyna*), 34
Heavy-hammer nut, see Hickory, Mockernut
Heron
  Black-crowned Night (*Nycticorax nycticorax*), 26, 79
  Great Blue (*Ardea herodias*), 151
  Yellow-crowned Night (*Nyctanassa violacea*), 67
Hickory
  Big Shagbark, see Shellbark Hickory
  Bitternut (*Carya cordiformis*), 42
  King Nut, see Shellbark Hickory
  Mockernut (*Carya tomentosa*), 42
  Pale (*Carya pallida*), 42, 167
  Pignut (*Carya glabra*), 42, 107
  Shagbark (*Carya ovata*), 42
  Shellbark (*Carya laciniosa*), 42

Small Pignut (*Carya ovalis*), 42
White-heart, see Mockernut Hickory
Honeysuckle, Japanese (*Lonicera Japonica*), 106
Hudsonia (*Hudsonia tomentosa*; *Hudsonia ericoides*), 91-92
Hummingbird, Ruby-throated (*Archilocus colubris*), 87
Hyssop (*Hyssopus officinalis*), 108

Ibis, Glossy (*Plegadis falcinellus*), 67

Jaeger, Parasitic (*Stercorarius parasiticus*), 129
Japanese Beetle (*Popillia japonica*), 106
Jay, Blue (*Cyanocitta cristata*), xiii, 23, 47, 50, 65, 76, 152
Joe-pye-weed (*Eupatorium fistulosum*), 35, 189
Junco, Slate-colored (*Junco hyemalis*), 150
Juncus effusus (Soft Rush), 24
Juniper
  Common (*Juniperus communis*), 108
  Ground (*Juniperus horizontalis*), 108

Kingbird, Eastern (*Tyrannus tyrannus*), 119
Kingfisher, Belted (*Megaceryle alcyon*), 151
Kinglet
  Golden-crowned (*Regulus satrapa*), 150
  Ruby-crowned (*Regulus calendula*), 150
Kite, Everglade (*Rostrhamus sociabilis*), 164
Kittiwake, Black-legged (*Rissa tridactyla*), 78, 129, 130, 158

Labrador Tea (*Ledum groenlandicum*), 59, 60, 150
Lad's Love (*Artemisia Abrotanum*), 108
Larch, American (*Larix laricina*), 59
Lark, Horned
  Hoyt's (*Eremophila alpestris hoyti*), 40
  Northern (*Eremophila a. alpestris*), 40, 157, 191
  Prairie (*Eremophila alpestris praticola*), 39-40
Lavender (*Lavendula officinalis*), 108 .

INDEX

Leatherleaf (*Chamaedaphne calyculata*), 60, 79
Lichen, Zoned (*Crocynia zonata*), 174
Lily
  Water (*Nymphaea odorata*), 85
  Wood (*Lilium philadelphicum*), 94
Lobelia
  Boykin's (*Lobelia Boykinii*), 79, 80
  Downy (*Lobelia puberula*), 167
Longspur, Lapland (*Calcarius lapponicum*), 40, 163

Maiden Cane (*Panicum hemitomon*), 79
Mandrake, see May Apple
Maple
  Mountain (*Acer spicatum*), 182
  Red (*Acer rubrum*), 23, 100
Marjoram (*Marjorana hortensis*), 108, 109
Marsh Cinquefoil (*Potentilla palustris*), 25
Marsh Elder (*Iva frutescens*), 167
Marsh Marigold (*Caltha palustris*), 60
Martin, Purple (*Progne subis*), 134
May Apple (*Podophyllum peltatum*), 33
Merganser, Common (*Mergus merganser*), 150, 151
Mermaid-weed (*Proserpinaca sp.*), 79
Mockingbird (*Mimus polyglottus*), *xiii, xvii,* 47, 49-50, 153, 188, 189
Moker-noot, see Hickory, Mockernut
Mole Cricket (subfamily Gryllotalpinae), 80-83
Mole Spurge (*Euphorbia Lathyris*), 114
Morning Glory, Pickering's (*Breweria Pickeringii*), 144
Moss
  Irish (*Chondrus crispus*), 158
  Reindeer (*Cladonia rangiferina*), 180
  Spanish (*Tillandsia usneoides*), 153, 165
Moss Pink (*Phlox subulata*), 108
Mullein
  Giant (*Verbascum Thapsus*), 114
  Moth (*Verbascum Blattaria*), 113
  White (*Verbascum Lychnitis*), 114
Murre
  Common (*Uria aalge*), 158
  Thick-billed (*Uria lomvia*), 130, 158
Muskgrass, see Chara
Myotis
  Keen (*Myotis keeni*), 110
  Little Brown (*Myotis lucifugus*), 110, 113
  Small-footed (*Myotis subulatus*), 110

Nighthawk, Common (*Chordeiles minor*), 117, 134
Nuthatch
  Red-breasted (*Sitta canadensis*), 132, 150
  White-breasted (*Sitta carolinensis*), 67
Nut-rush, 45

Oak
  Basket (*Quercus Michauxii*), 86, 100, 167
  Bearcat (*Quercus ilicifolia*), 86, 182
  Black (*Quercus velutina*), 86, 145
  Black Jack (*Quercus marilandica*), 86, 145
  Chestnut (*Quercus Prinus*), 177
  Cow, see Basket Oak
  Dwarf Chestnut (*Quercus prinoides*), 86
  Laurel (*Quercus laurifolia*), 167
  Live (*Quercus virginiana*), 153
  Over-cup, see Swamp Post Oak
  Pin (*Quercus palustris*), 86, 94
  Poison (*Rhus Toxicodendron*), 145
  Post (*Quercus stellata*), 86, 145, 180
  Red (*Quercus rubra*), 86
  Rudkin's (*XQuercus Rudkini*), 145
  Scarlet (*Quercus coccinea*), 86, 145, 155, 181
  Shingle (*Quercus imbricaria*), 145
  Spanish (*Quercus falcata*), 78, 86, 139, 145, 167
  Swamp Post (*Quercus lyrata*), 85, 86, 144
  Swamp White (*Quercus bicolor*), 86, 94
  Water (*Quercus nigra*), 139, 167
  White (*Quercus alba*), 34, 86, 145
  Willow (*Quercus Phellos*), 86, 145, 167
  Yellow (*Quercus Muhlenbergii*), 137
Orange Amanita, see Agaric, Royal
Orchis
  Cranefly (*Tipularia discolor*), 167
  Grass-pink (*Calopogon pulchellus*), 183
  Snowy (*Habenaria nivea*), 167

INDEX

Oriole
  Baltimore (*Icterus galbula*), 26, 30
  Orchard (*Icterus spurius*), 25, 33, 35
Osage Orange (*Maclura pomifera*), 105, 187
Osprey (*Pandion haliaetus*), xiii, 139
Our Lady's Bedstraw (*Galium verum*), 109
Ovenbird, see Teacher-bird
Owl
  Barn (*Tyto alba*), 171
  Barred (*Strix varia*), 171
  Great Horned (*Bubo virginiana*), 106, 131, 171-172
  Long-eared (*Asio otus*), 107
  Sawwhet (*Aegolius acadicus*), 107, 171
  Screech (*Otus asio*), 171, 172
  Short-eared (*Asio flammeus*), 139
  Snowy (*Nyctea scandiaca*), 158
Oystercatcher, American (*Haematopus palliatus*), 138, 163

Parsnip
  Cow (*Heracleum maximum*), 28
  Water (*Sium suave*), 93
Peeper, Spring (*Hyla crucifer*), 195
Pennyroyal (*Mentha pulegium*), 108
Pennyroyal, False (*Hedeoma pulegioides*), 128
Penstemon, 190
Persimmon (*Diospyros virginiana*), 78
Petrel, Wilson's Storm (*Oceanites oceanicus*), xviii, 130
Pewee, Eastern Wood (*Contopus virens*), 87
Phoebe, Eastern (*Sayornis phoebe*), 29-33
Pickerelweed (*Pontederia cordata*), 93
Pine
  Austrian (*Pinus nigra*), 105
  Florida Slash (*Pinus elliottii*), 153, 165
  Loblolly (*Pinus taeda*), 100, 167
  Pitch (*Pinus rigida*), 99, 100, 139, 166, 179, 180
  Pond (*Pinus serotina*), 100
  Spruce (*Pinus glabra*), 165
  Virginia (*Pinus virginiana*), 100, 177
  White (*Pinus Strobus*), 23, 156
  Yellow (*Pinus echinata*), 166, 179, 181

Pinxter Flower (*Rhododendron nudiflorum*), 34
Pipistrelle, Eastern (*Pipistrellus subflavus*), 110
Pipit, Water (*Anthus spinoletta*), 191
Pitcher Plant (*Sarracenia purpurea*), 60, 91
Plover
  American Golden (*Pluvialis dominica*), 191
  Black-bellied (*Squatarola squatarola*), 191
  Piping (*Charadrius melodus*), 164
  Upland (*Bartramia longicauda*), 27
  Wilson's (*Charadrius wilsonia*), 138
Poison Hemlock (*Conium maculatum*), 28
Poison Ivy (*Rhus radicans*), 79, 92
Prunus
  Avium, see Cherry, Sweet
  Cerasus, see Cherry, Sour
  depressa, see Cherry, Sand
  susquehanae, 98
Puffin, Common (*Fratercula arctica*), 130, 158
Purple Loosestrife (*Lythrum Salicaria*), 36, 37
Pyrola, 94
Pyxie Moss (*Pyxidanthera barbulata*), 91, 179

Queen Anne's Lace (*Daucus carota*), 23, 27, 35, 38

Rail
  Black (*Laterallus jamaicensis*), xix, 106, 178, 179
  Clapper (*Rallus longirostris*), 179
Rat, Norway (*Rattus norvegicus*), 106
Rattlesnake
  Canebrake (*Crotalus horridus atricaudus*), 116, 153
  Pigmy (*Sistrurus miliarius*), 153
  Timber (*Crotalus h. horridus*), 116
Raven, Common (*Corvus corax*), 158
Redpoll, Common (*Acanthis flammea*), 40, 48
Redstart, American (*Setophaga ruticilla*), 26, 35, 87, 196
Reeve, see Ruff
Rhodora (*Rhododendron canadense*), 150
River Rocket, see Yellow Rocket
River Salad, see Yellow Rocket
Robin (*Turdus migratorius*), 26, 29, 33, 97, 105, 187

INDEX

Rock polypody (*Polypodium virginianum*), 177
Rose Mallow (*Hibiscus palustris*), 79, 167
Rosemary (*Rosmarinus officinalis*), 108
Rose of Sharon (*Hibiscus syriacus*), 29
Rose Pink (*Sabatia angularis*), 38, 39
Ruff (*Philomachus pugnax*), 191

Saint John's-wort (*Hypericum punctatum*), 24
Sanderling (*Crocethia alba*), 84, 163
Sand Myrtle (*Leiophyllum buxifolium*), 91, 179
Sandpiper
  Buff-breasted (*Tryngites subruficollis*), 191
  Lead-back, see Dunlin
  Least (*Erolia minutilla*), 84
  Pectoral (*Erolia melanotus*), 67
  Purple (*Erolia maritima*), 78, 164
  Red-back, see Dunlin
  Semipalmated (*Ereunetes pusillus*), xix, 84
  Western (*Ereunetes mauri*), 84
  White-rumped (*Erolia fuscicolles*), 84
Sandwort, Pine Barren (*Arenaria caroliniana*), 179
scaup, 77
Sea Pink (*Sabatia stellaris*), 163, 167
Shadbush (*Amelanchier arborea*), 28
Shearwater, Manx (*Puffinus puffinus*), 130
Shrike
  Loggerhead, see Migrant Shrike
  Migrant (*Lanius ludovicianus*), 153, 188, 189
Siskin, Pine (*Spinus pinus*), 48, 159-160
Skua, Great (*Catharacta skua*), 129, 130, 131
Skylark (*Alauda arvensis*), 39
Snake
  Black Racer (*Coluber constrictor*), 115, 183
  Eastern Garter (*Thamnophis sirtalis*), 115
  Eastern Milk (*Lampropeltis doliata triangulum*), 23, 24, 115
  Northern Pine (*Pituophis m. melanoleucus*), 179-181
Sneezeweed (*Helenium nudiflorum*), 189

Snipe, Wilson's (Common) (*Capella gallinago*), 83
Sora (*Porzana carolina*), 26
Sparrow
  Atlantic Song (*Melospiza melodia atlantica*), 163
  Chipping (*Spizella passerina*), 30, 61, 70, 132
  English (*Passer domesticus*), 48, 179
  Field (*Spizella pusilla*), 27, 61
  Grasshopper (*Ammodramus savannarum*), 25
  Ipswich (*Passerculus princeps*), 163
  Song (*Melospiza melodia*), xix, 47, 61, 105, 163
  Tree (*Spizella arborea*), 47, 61
  Vesper (*Poecetus gramineus*), 163
  White-throated (*Zonotrichia albicollis*), 47, 61, 132, 150
Spatterdock (*Nuphar advena*), 93
Spikemoss
  Meadow (*Selaginella apoda*), 24, 25
  Rock (*Selaginella rupestris*), 25, 178
Spleenwort
  Brownstem (*Asplenium platyneuron*), 177
  Maidenhair (*Asplenium trichomanes*), 177
Spring Cress (*Cardamine bulbosa*), 28
Spruce
  Black (*Picea mariana*), 60, 157
  Norway (*Picea Abies*), 105
  Red (*Picea rubens*), 127, 128, 149, 150
Squaw-weed, see Golden Ragwort
Squirrel
  Eastern Gray (*Sciurus carolinensis*), 48
  Red (*Tamiasciurus hudsonicus*), 48
Stagger Weed, see Wild Bleeding Heart
Star Flower (*Trientalis borealis*), 94
Starling (*Sturnus vulgaris*), 54, 105, 106, 179
Stonewort, see Chara
Strawberry Bush (*Euonymus americanus*), 167
Sumac, Poison (*Rhus Vernix*), 23, 25, 41
Swallow
  Bank (*Riparia riparia*), 117, 134
  Barn (*Hirundo rustica*), 26, 30, 117
  Rough-winged (*Stelgidopteryx ruficollis*), 134
  Tree (*Iridoprocne bicolor*), 117, 134
Swamp Pink, see Arethusa

INDEX

Swan, Mute (*Cygnus olor*), 151
Sweet Cicely (*Osmorhiza Claytoni*), 28
Swift, Chimney (*Chaetura pelagica*), 37, 117
Sycamore (*Platanus occidentalis*), 26, 172

Tanager, Scarlet (*Piranga olivacea*), 26, 35
Tarragon (*Artemisia Dracunculus*), 108
Teacher-bird (Ovenbird) (*Seiurus aurocapillus*), 26, 34
Teal, European (Common) (*Anas crecca*), 191
Tent Caterpillar (*Malacosoma americana*), 97
Tern
  Arctic (*Sterna paradisea*), 129
  Forster's (*Sterna forsteri*), 138
  Gull-billed (*Gelochelidon nilotica*), 138
  Roseate (*Sterna dougallii*), 138
Thrush
  Bicknell's (*Hylocichla minima bicknelli*), 132
  Golden-crowned, see Teacher-bird
  Hermit (*Hylocichla guttata*), 132
  Olive-back (Swainson's) (*Hylocichla ustulata*), 132
  Wood (*Hylocichla mustelina*), 25, 50, 106, 132
Thyme (*Thymus vulgaris*), 108
Tickseed (*Coreopsis rosea*), 86
Timothy (*Phleum pratense*), 23, 105
Titmouse, Tufted (*Parus bicolor*), xvii, 26, 154, 187
Torreya, Florida (*Torreya taxifolia*), 154
Trillium, Nodding (*Trillium cernuum*), 93
Tulip tree (*Liriodendron tulipfera*), 100
Turkey Beard (*Xerophyllum asphodeloides*), 91-92
Turkey Corn, see Wild Bleeding Heart
Turtle
  Eastern Painted (*Chrysemis p. picta*), 196
  Muhlenberg's Bog (*Clemmys muhlenbergi*), 183-184

Veery (*Hylocichla fuscescens*), 25, 94, 132
Viburnum, Rafinesque's (*Viburnum Rafinesquianum*), 137

Violet
  Florida (*Viola floridana*), 165
  Lance-leaved (*Viola lanceolata*), 94
  Marsh (*Viola cucullata*), 28
Vireo
  Philadelphia (*Vireo philadelphicus*), 149
  Solitary (*Vireo solitarius*), 149
  Warbling (*Vireo gilvus*), 35, 67
  Yellow-throated (*Vireo flavifrons*), 27
Vulture, Turkey (*Cathartes aura*), xvii, 23, 117, 187

Warbler
  Bay-breasted (*Dendroica castanea*), 35
  Black and White (*Mniotilta varia*), 35
  Blackburnian (*Dendroica fusca*), 35, 149
  Blackpoll (*Dendroica striata*), 33, 35, 149
  Black-throated Blue (*Dendroica caerulescens*), 35
  Black-throated Green (*Dendroica virens*), 35, 132
  Blue-winged (*Vermivora pinus*), 35
  Canada (*Wilsonia canadensis*), 26, 35
  Cape May (*Dendroica tigrina*), 35, 87
  Cerulean (*Dendroica caerulea*), 26, 35
  Chestnut-sided (*Dendroica pensylvanica*), 26, 35
  Hooded (*Wilsonia citrina*), 35
  Kentucky (*Oporornis formosus*), 26, 35
  Lawrence's (*XVermivora lawrencei*), 35
  Mourning (*Oporornis philadelphia*), 35, 131, 133, 150
  Myrtle (*Dendroica coronata*), 35, 61, 132, 149, 164
  Nashville (*Vermivora ruficapilla*), 35
  Orange-crowned (*Vermivora celata*), 34
  Palm (*Dendroica palmarum*), 34
  Parula (*Parula americana*), 165
  Pine (*Dendroica pinus*), 34, 92
  Prairie (*Dendroica discolor*), 92
  Prothonotary (*Protonotaria citrea*), 35, 187
  Tennessee (*Vermivora peregrina*), 35
  Wilson's (*Wilsonia pusilla*), 35, 87

INDEX

Yellow (*Dendroica petechia*), 24, 26, 105
Yellow-throated (*Dendroica dominica*), 35
Water-hemp (*Acnida cannabina*), 167
Water Starwort (*Callitriche heterophylla*), 80, 93
Water-thrush, Louisiana (*Seirus motacilla*), 27, 34
Waxwing, Cedar (*Bombycilla cedrorum*), 87
Whale, Pilot (*Globicephala ventricosa*), 130
Wild Bleeding Heart (*Dicentra eximia*), 127
Wild Carrot, see Queen Anne's Lace
Wild Marjoram (*Origanum vulgare*), 109
Wild Plum (*Prunus americana*), 28
Wild Thyme (*Thymus serpyllum*), 108, 109
Winterberry (*Ilex verticillata*), 23
Witherod (*Viburnum cassinoides*), 93
Woodcock, American (*Philohela minor*), 83
Woodpecker
   American Three-toed (*Picoides tridactylus*), 148
   Downy (*Dendrocopus pubescens*), 47
   Hairy (*Dendrocopus villosus*), 152
   Ivory-billed (*Campephilus principalis*), 166

   Pileated (*Dryocopus pileatus*), 165
   Red-bellied (*Centurus carolinus*), xvii, 187
   Red-headed (*Melanerpes erythrocephalus*), xvii, 153
Woodrat, Eastern (*Neotoma floridana*), 195
Wren
   Carolina (*Thryothorus ludovicianus*), xvii
   House (*Troglodytes aedon*), 26, 30, 37, 38
   Long-billed Marsh (*Telmatodytes palustris*), 24
   Winter (*Troglodytes troglodytes*), 34, 132, 150

Xerces Society, xv

Yarrow, Common (*Achillea Millefolium*), 23
Yellow Rocket (*Barbarea vulgaris*), 27
Yellow-throat (*Geothlypis trichas*), 24, 26, 35, 70, 87
Yellow-throat, Maryland, see Yellow-throat
Yellow-throat, Northern, see Yellow-throat
Yew, Florida (*Taxus floridana*), 154